THE NUER NATION:

SOCIO-ECONOMIC AND CULTURAL CHANGE

Gabriel Gai Riam

The publisher wishes to acknowledge and thank Dr. Douglas H. Johnson for his invaluable help and support for Africa World Books and its mission of preserving and promoting African cultural and literary traditions and history. Dr. Johnson and fellow historians have been instrumental in ensuring that African people remain connected to their past and their identity. Africa World Books is proud to carry on this mission.

Cover design, typesetting and layout: Africa World Books
Unit 3, 57 Frobisher St, Osborne Park, WA 6017
P.O. Box 1106 Osborne Park, WA 6916

Mold of Nuer Home Estate with cows at the barn (byre):

Photo by the author

MAP OF NUER NATION (*ROL NATH*): SHOWING ADMINISTRATIVE COUNTIES

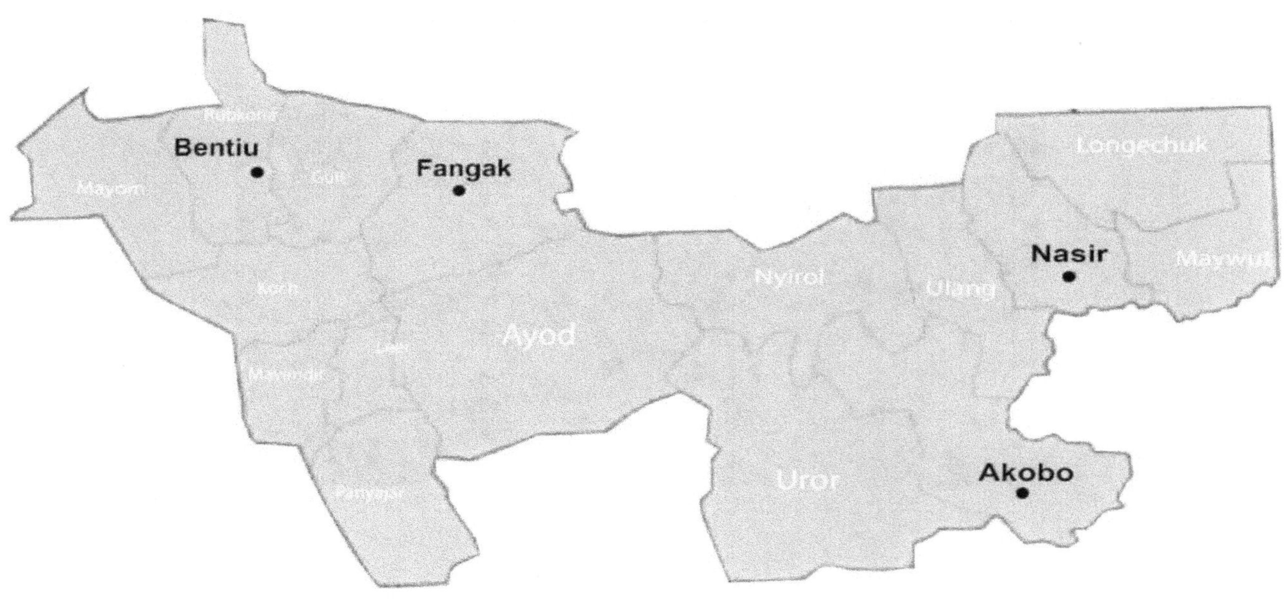

DEDICATION

This text is dedicated to the Nuer people in South Sudan, Ethiopia and the Diaspora. This contribution serves as a wakeup call for all the Nuer people and other South Sudanese nationalities keen on reviving their cultures.

ACKNOWLEDGEMENT

First and foremost, I wish to thank those who have made it possible to write about the Nuer people of South Sudan. A special thanks is owed to Prof. Douglas H. Johnson, who has provided useful materials for writing this text. A sincere appreciation goes to Prof. Francis Owino Rew, who has been a careful reader of the manuscript, and has contributed in numerous ways to its final form and content. I am also grateful to Dr. Awet Arang, Chol Martin and Amb Dhano Ajak for their encouragement and professional support in inspiring me to conclude this text.

I am indebted to all the Nuer community members who have spared their time through group discussions and individual conversations, particularly; Revds. Matthew M. Deng, Paul Bol Kuel, Joseph Nhial Hoth, Kuong Ninrew Dong, Biel Malou, Elder Buay, Hon. John Mayual Nguot, Chuol Rambang Luoth, Hoth Mai Nguth, John Kong Nyuon, Dr. James Mabor Gatkuoth, Elder James Sigin Banak, Rev Michael Aban, Tut Wakow Gang,Tut Riek Luak, Koang Bar Malieth, Stephen Tut Poul, Gai Wuor Ker and Mai Riek Luak, other community elders: Pouk Radheal, Chuol Diu Teny, Moses Mayul Thor and Moses Dop Hoth, special thanks is owed to Kuong Ter Duol, Ms Lydia Nyange and my driver Baros Mubaraka Atem, all of whom provided useful contributions to the quality of this text.

Finally, I dearly thank my wife Marina Riam and children: Nyakor, late Riam, Nyawejok, Emmanuel, Nyakueth and Rejoice for their encouragement, patience and financial sustenance throughout the drafting process of this text.

TABLE OF CONTENTS

LIST OF FIGURES

ABBREVIATIONS

AIR:	African Indigenous Religions
APS:	African Political Systems
ATB:	African Traditional Believers
ATR:	African Traditional Religion
BCE:	Before Christian Era
CUEA:	The Catholic University of Eastern Africa
CE:	Common Era
DC:	District Commissioner
DCs:	District Commissioners
DNA:	Deoxyribonucleic Acid
EN:	Eastern Nilotic
ICH:	Intangible Culture Heritage
IDPs:	Internally Displaced Persons
KJV:	King James Version, published in 1613 by Robert Barker in London.
MCTD:	Master Culture, Theology and Development
MIR:	Military Intelligence Report
MPA:	Master in Public Administration
MMR:	Mix Methodology Research
MCTD:	Master, Culture, Theology and Development
NAS:	National Salvation Front
NIF:	National Islamic Front
N.C.Os:	None Commission Officers
NDCs:	Nuer District Commissioners
NIV:	New International Version, published in 1978 by Biblical United States, Palmer Lake, Colorado.
NTL:	New Living Translation, published in 1996 by Tyndale House Foundation located in Carol Stream, Illinois.
PCoSS:	Presbyterian Church of South Sudan
SN:	Southern Nilotic
TCSS:	The Transitional Constitution of South Sudan
UK:	United Kingdom
WN:	Western Nilotic

A GLOSSARY OF NUER WORDS AND PHRASES

Bieer:	Tattoos,
Cääk:	Creator,
Cholwic:	*A* person who died in abnormal circumstance such as struck, killed by elephant, disappeared beyond trace whose spirit is believed to appear at sunrise or sunset
Cieŋ Naath:	Nuer homeland
Däpäny:	Tower of Babel (Incomplete building), Heavenly place where the dawn when scarifies are offered
Dhoom:	Adultery
Duol diitni:	Council of Nuer elders?
Gäär:	Six or seven facial markings beforehand into adulthood
Gäri:	Initiation transition process to adulthood
Gol:	Family
Gook:	Prophets
Ɣoth:	Transhumance
Kaar:	Lineage
Këëth:	The urine of cow
Koat Lich:	Tamarind tree where the Nuer originated or believe they or were created in Liech area - Jagei
KuärTuac:	Leopard-Skin Chief
Kuär Biey:	Government appointed chief
Kuel jiakni:	Tree of Bad Things (on which, body of Prophet Guek was hanged)
Kuer Kuong:	The birth place of the Nuer Nation as a distinct ethnic group
Kuoth nhial:	God in the sky
Kuoth:	God
Luy:	Homicide
Maar:	Kinship
Mäi:	Dry season
Mat Nuärä:	Nuer Unity
Naath:	Plural form of Nuer which refers to all mankind which is linked to Biblical creation
Nak lɛc:	Removing of lower teeth
ŋäth:	Manifestation
ŋuɔt:	Laws or rules (plural form) of *ŋut*
ŋut:	Covenant (singular form)
Nhial:	Meaning rain or sky
Nueer:	Meaning contamination or sins
Nuer:	Invented name that replaced Naath
Pälikä:	Forgiveness
Piil:	Small flat stone for grinding grain
Pëth:	Evil eye/wizard

Ran:	Meaning individual "person as distinct from other ethnic communities ("People")
Ri̱ic:	Nuer age-set
Ruic:	Leadership (authority)
Rool Naath:	Nuer Land
Thiliaka/Thiak:	Humility
Thok Naath:	Nuer language
Thuok:	Honesty (fact/truth)
Tiët:	Witchcraft
Töny lääŋ:	A brass pipe of Prophet Ngundɛŋ
Tɔt:	Rainy season
Tutgäär:	Super-Being that makes an important point in the Nuer worldview – another name for God
Twɔc Ɣok:	Dowry through negotiation processes
Wän/kueel:	Thief
Yaŋ:	Cow
Yier Känychäŋ:	East of the Nile

PREFACE

"[The Nuer] still remain a very remarkable people; tough, resilient deeply democratic… They strut about as the Lords of the earth, which indeed they consider themselves to be" (Evans - Prichard 1927-1973).

At the time of writing this text there were political upheavals in many parts of Africa, particularly in countries served by the River Nile: Egypt had earlier suffered the 'Arab uprising' with coups and counter coups; the Sudan was in turmoil following the overthrow of Al Bashir and the actors in the removal of the despot remain at each other's' throats for inclusion in the management of the country. The youngest state in Africa, South Sudan, has not settled raging squabbles of leadership turning the freedom from the hostile Arab north to a mockery of the hard earned independence Guns and smoke are still the order of the day in northern Uganda and eastern Democratic Republic of the Congo. Along the Blue Nile the strife in Ethiopia has left residents in the Eastern part of the South Sudan uneasy as they receive droves of refugees fleeing from the battle between the Ethiopian government soldiers and the rebels in the Tigray region.

All these, as has been the case throughout Africa, trigger a need to document the experiences of the communities affected. The Nuer story has been documented largely by foreign settlers. However, such writings have not had the advantage of the first-hand experience of the socio-economic and cultural life of the community.

The present writer is a native of Nuer people from South Sudan, who underwent many experiences during the colonization periods including narrowly escaping the massacres that took place in Akobo County South Sudan where many people were killed in 1970. Earlier in 1965 Arab soldiers attacked the community in Renk County killing and maiming several merely because the Nuer, along with other southern communities agitated for freedom from the hostile administration of the Arab north.

During the second civil war (1983 – 2005), I was involved in relief work among the refugees in Southern Sudan, Kenya and in United Kingdom, an experience that exposed me to many other challenges as well before proceeding to further studies in the UK and Kenya where I earned Masters and Doctor of Philosophy: Master in Public Administration (MPA); Master in Culture, Theology and Development (MCTD) and Master of Philosophy - MPhil. Both inquiries had involved Christianity, Islamic themes alongside African indigenous religion from which my interest in writing my first book *Christian-Muslim Relations in Sudan* arose. An interest that continued when pursuing my doctoral degree at The Catholic University of Eastern Africa (CUEA). I presented several papers in Nuer culture, Arabisation and forced Islamisation in South Sudan. Each essay had a consideration of some more detailed on how Nuer culture has been affected.

Questions may arise naturally whether there is such a thing as progress and whether one can construct a coherent and directional Nuer history. Socio-economic and cultural changes have kept the Nuer too busy to consider the questions for the bigger part of this Century. The fading of Nuer culture in the 21st Century comes to invite and raise queries about old Nuer traditions one more time. These factors later form representative sample in collecting information in Nuer society. I have chosen and adopted Mixed Methodology Research (MMR) for gathering information: secondary and primary data collection; conducted interviews with individuals; group discussions and personal observations since 2018. It was not easy though to accomplish this work in the midst of political war situations, yet it was important to press on for the goal and reached out to the participants who have influenced the outcome of this text.

Although, Nuer people have been enshrined in the anthropological wisdom by Prof. Evans-Prichard from the 1930s, they continue to fascinate, despite the challenges affecting their moral values as they interact with other cultures and other forms of influences relevant to modernization and change. As such, these contributions are some of the most stimulating developments which require documentation in recent times. There is still no reliable textbook on Nuer comprehensively covering all the structures of their system beside this text. Although text might suffer a degree of brevity that does not do justice to some important topics that ought to have been elaborated, readers will have to contend with the text in its form. It has not been possible to address all the necessary issues left unconnected by the previous scholars. However, new developments seeking answers have emerged: Christianity, Islam and Indigenous African Nuer have been problematic. Also the patterns of Nuer migration due to wars and conflicts remain areas of research, while there is also an opportunity to learn more about Nuer people in this changing environment and how they fit into the wider community of South Sudan and the world at large.

INTRODUCTION

A lot has been written about the Nuer, but the early writers left confounding facts about the community. Late Prof. Evans-Pritchard who reluctantly accepted to work among the Nuer became the pioneer and later the most famous scholar whom the academic world would recognize. His classic investigations made the Nuer one of the most confounding peoples in the ethnographic literature. Late Prof. Howell compiled a manual of Nuer Law that accounted for most of the Nuer Customary Law Courts, its evolution and development was important because it came as a result of the Nuer District Commissioners' meetings first conducted in 1943, a change that was deemed necessary to avert the existed Nuer egalitarian system. Douglas Johnson took the lead to investigate more about the Nuer Prophets from the Upper Nile region of South Sudan in the mid-1970s. He remains one of the outstanding scholars who attempted to promote African cultures. The late Professor Giet Jal had earlier presented the history of South Sudan's Jikäny of eastern Nuer Ethnic Groups between 1500 and 1920, partly covering the migration period of Jikäny Nuer. Late Dr. Wall Duany projects the Nuer as an acceplous society having neither palaces nor prisons in their governing system. Sharon Hutchinson, in her book the Nuer Dilemmas: Coping with Money, War, and the State, reveals and describes how the Nuer have challenged the extreme thoughtful moral, social and political in their war and conflict situations.

Although these early writers laid a foundation on the knowledge about the Nuer, gaps remain to be filled. Since those writings lots of socio-economic and cultural changes have emerged. A text such as the current one is an attempt to fill the gaps through research and interviews among a people who are living in permanent settlements under new government free from north Sudan interference.

Nuer have undergone a great socio-economic and cultural transformation since their southward migrations. These changes are illuminated in the text as similarities with other Nilotic groups also addressed. The text traces the origin of the Nuer people, where they live and delves into their genes that sets them apart from the other Nilotic communities. The text is written with the hope that it will contribute to the Nuer understanding of their culture and become a measure of creative thinking, inspiring element in the current challenging times. As we count down our days toward the horizon, catching up with ages, something memorable to the Nuer Nation should be done before the dawn bids us bye. To unpack these facts of wisdom, values and drastic changes noted in the text will later on speak by themselves to South Sudanese people and the academia. Therefore, the study pattern of this text about the Nuer socio-economic and cultural change should strikingly reveal and unpack new grounds which could be applied for the study of other Nilotic ethnic groups, who might have similar cultural trends as in South Sudan and beyond.

CHAPTER ONE:
ORIGIN AND SETTLEMENT

Myth of creation and origin

The story of the origin of the Nuer is captured in the myth of *koat Liech* (Tamarind tree) - *tuk naath* tradition centers on a famous tamarind tree. Tamarind tree is a symbol of social and genealogical representation of the Nuer practices associated with founding ancestors in origin stories among many Nuer communities. The tree is perceived as a communal symbols, of the Nuer communities; past, present and future, is seen as creating peoples by gathering them under and around the tree. This story of *koat Liech* is also connected with the myth of a rope that is believed to have been connecting earth and the sky. Some Nuer elders described how the Gaawäär ancestors came down from the sky to settle in the west one by one, just as their people later crossed the river to settle in the east 'bit by bit' (Johnson, 2016). Most Nuer believe that *koat Liech* was the place where the ancestors of the Nuer and other people first appeared. Even though the original tree no longer exists, the site is still sacred, a place for offerings sacrifices. It is also a place where people got separated and migrated to other areas of the South that later became part of Nuer nation. Myths and legends, comprise both religious and historical explanations about Nuer societies.

In the most basic forms of the tale, two "brothers" named Ɣääk and Gëë came together under a particular tamarind tree called *koat* on the west bank of the Nile and at this sacred tree they cut a bull in half (from head to tail) to prohibit "incest" (*ruaal*) between their offspring's. They also agreed that this tree had to be fixed as a boundary between the "descendants" of Ɣääk to the south and those of Gëë to the north. Given that Nuer use the same rite to address incest that they also say marked the "beginning of people" (*tuk Naath*) as a story about redefining bonds of kinship and transforming ordinary "humans" (*raan*) into beings morally valid as "people" (*naath*) whose exogamous relationships made them Nuer. This tradition explains that Ɣääk and Gëë, were the first "people" (*naath*), descendants of "*Ran*, (human) whose father is said to be *kwoth* (God). They argue that human beings pre-dated *Koat-Liech*. Taken as a whole, these traditions actually declare that divinity created Homo sapiens (the species to which all modern human beings belong) sometime before Gëë and Ɣää*k* but that it was these particular ancestors who created meaningful history (*tuk naath*) by inventing a kind of exogamous kinship. We have noticed above, similar myth about Nuer elders inventing incest at "*Kuer Kuong*" at the time they started migrated south from Kordofan around 1700"), but there was no mentioned of any specific place or sign such like "shrine" where stopping incest was performed, that people could easily referred to. Both tales give possibility for further investigation. Thus, *kuer kuong* myths felt short of indicating Nuer (Naath) were first created. Similarly, the version, *Koat Liech* leaves a vacuum for another distinct origin of the Eastern Jikäny Nuer tale which hinges on a famous ancestor named *Kiir*, known as *kiir kaker* (gotten from "gourd").

From this mythology, the settlement of the community and attendant cultural references thereafter can be understood. The Nuer Nation occupy a huge territory both from the west and east of the Nile in South Sudan with a small portion in Ethiopia belonging to Nilotic language groups. The Nuer are agro-pastoralists who herd cattle for a living. The cattle are the most

1

important assets and serve as companions and define their lifestyle. They also practice fishing and cultivate sorghum and maize. This pattern of the Nuer economy can be called "pastoral-agrico-fishing" society. This shows how the three operators work in economic life of the Nuer society and the link of values of agriculture, livestock and fishing practices. The combination of these three modes of life can be assumed to have changed the Nuer society over the years. The Nuer called themselves Naath as they were continuously oppressed by the ruling foreign invaders in their homeland affecting traditions and culture. Traditional sources indicate that Nuer birth place was *Kuer Kuoŋ* where they developed sanctions before moving southward and settled in western Upper Nile – Bentiu as their "homeland" where they later on parted ways and migrated to the east of the Nile which they called "*kiir känycäŋ*". They have a consistent oral tradition indicating that their expansion across the Nile, as far as the Ethiopian border, has a 200-year legacy. In the process of this expansion, they forced the Anyuak to migrate further east into western Ethiopia and incorporated many Anyuak, Dinka and Burun into Nuer communities. As Johnson (2016) noted, the segmentary societies of Dinka and Nuer were able to incorporate foreign individuals and foreign lineages. The environment of the eastern plains are such that any place that could support permanent settlement was then occupied by a mixed population, and their long-term survival depended on establishing links between groups pursuing different livelihood strategies in different ecological places that involved the strategy of building 'wealth-in-people, and political power based on this strategy depended (Johnson, 2016).

The Nuer people were once independent before the coming of colonizers. They had control and freedom over their own politically defined world which they called "*Rol Naath*". A homogenous state, with social hierarchy and temporal base like events relevant to appropriate time and person to do the tasks such as that of the British Common Laws emerged. The Nuer are traditionally divided into three regional federations: the western Nuer residing west of Bhar el Jebel, the central of Zeraf Velly Nuer comprising the Lak, Thiang and Gaawäär and the Eastern Nuer which includes; Lou and Eastern Jikäny. The Atwot group have been historically part of the Nuer homeland but have moved towards the status of a separate cultural group (Raymond, 1985). They were formerly a section of the Nuer occupying the present border between the Jagei and Dok Nuer in the west of the Nile. Nuer traditions hold that the Atwot migrated southward as a result of conflicts with other Nuer groups. However, Atwot migration and causes of their conflicts lie outside the scope of this text.

The Nuer originally are said to have been a section of other people that migrated out of low land into a desert land which they then called "*Kuer Kuoŋ*", located in southern Kordofan currently old name around 1700. After centuries of seclusion and influence from Luo peoples triggered them to be a distinct ethnic group from Naath. *Kuer Kuoŋ* was a dry land, unsuitable for livestock, crops production and encourage people to move to swamps where they could cultivate and graze their livestock (Seligman, 1932). Naath believed that within their environment there were animals that existed, and were created into the environment. The influx of Baggara Arabs and their subsequent slave raids into the area (*kuer kuong),* caused the Nuer to migrate further south and settled in Bentiu subsequently named South Sudan, which became the Nuer home. In this process, many Dinka were later absorbed into the Nuer culture so that the Nuer people are similar to the Dinka in aspects of culture and language. While many scholars such as Pritchard (1956), Johnson, (1980), Kelly (1985) & Stringham (2016) state that most Nuer have a Dinka background, others believe that Nuer have a Luo origin as well. Subsequently, *"Kuer Kuong"* was the birth place of the Nuer Nation as a distinct group of people after which the term "Nuer" was then invented as a means of sanction replacing the term *"Naath"* gradually. Another important term is *"Nuäär"* commonly use by Nuer themselves, as well as by their neighbors such as Dinka and Shilluk.

The three terms; "Nuer, Naath and Nuäär" are interchangeably used by the Nuer in their social lives, although the term Nuer is more commonly used than Naath and Nuäär. There has been confusion as to whether these terms; "Nuer, Naath and Nuäär" have different meanings given their effects on the various cultures they have interacted with. This text elucidates this misperception. However, Nuer is commonly use term than the Naath and Nuäär by foreigners and other South Sudanese ethnic communities. During the colonial periods to the present time, the term was used by Anglo–Egyptian Administration, the Sudan government and the government of South Sudan. They use the term Nuer to represent the ethnic community and it has been part of the records including the National Identification Cards, Birth Certificates and the National Passports. Within the Nuer community, Naath and Nuäär are known to be the names that signify the people who were later to be called Nuer. Both terms carry significant meaning (Kim, 2017). The concept of the terms "Naath" and the "Nuer" and their sanction centuries of usage within the periods of migration many years ago is believed to be related to migration of many tribes (communities) from Egypt, Sudan, Southern Kordofan (*Kuer Kuong*), Bhar el Ghazal and Western Upper Nile-Bentiu to *Koat Liech* (currently Unity State, Central and Eastern Nuer in the republic of South Sudan.

Some scholars such as Seligman (1932) and Cheikh Anto Diop (1981) argue that the term "Naath" existed long before and that the Naath is the old tradition name that carries not only personality of the people but also who these people were, as 'the Nuer themselves speak of the tribe (community) of the west of Bhar el Ghazal as 'Nuer homeland' (*Cieng Naath).* This indicates that the term Naath existed before and was widely used. Seligman, maintains that the country of the Nuer was *Kuer Kuoŋ;* the barren place of Kuoŋ, referring to the departure point where Nilotic departed from. Senegalese Egyptologist Diop noted the same, stating that Nuer true name is Naath and not Nuer. But Egyptians chose *Naas* or *Nahaas* to the Nubians and other blacks of Africans at the time. The Egyptians used the expression to distinguish the Nubians for blacks and Nahas is the name of the people with no color connotation in Egypt. With these arguments, *Thok Naath* is not a term that is confined to the Naath (Nuer) people of South Sudan.

It is believed that the language they used has connection to humanity and this language was the Naath language or Thok Naath. Archeologists dug up the evidences that show the spot of Tower of Babel. Their findings indicated that Tower of Babel (*Däpäny*) did in fact exist. Tower of Babel, in biblical literature was built in the land Shinar (Bablonia) - Iraq sometime after the Deluge. The building had 153 feet high with 400-foot base, constructed with bricks in seven stages to correspond with the outer planets. It was meant to be a place where the astrology or things of heaven such as the moon, stars, and the sun would be worshipped. "*Dä*" means destroy and "*päny*" means incomplete building in Nuer language. The two words means building that was destroyed before it could be completed and that was what is believed to be the Tower of Babel as narrated in (Genesis 11: 1-9). Some of the Nuer/Naath elders recognize that Tower of Babel was "*Däpäny*", known to be the dwelling place of gods as the bible explair (see appendix 1).).

The fall of Tower of Babel resulted in family and community units drifting away and developing distinctive cultures with different physical and biological characteristics. They were to communicate only with their own family units. Marrying outside the family was not possible. It was then necessary to establish new families composed of closed relatives that lasted for several generations (Kim, 2017). Since then, the issue of incest and other negative practices such as killing or murdering a neighbour became major concerns among the *Naath* people when they first settled at *Kuer Kuong* where they started to develop their laws (*nguɔt*) and invented the term "Nuer".

Traditional sources indicate that Nuer is the latest invented term drawn from the term "Nueer" (meaning contamination) created by group of elders at *Kuer Kuong* as part of their governing institutions. Nueer was meant for future generations to keep the laws (*Nguɔt*) in their social lives, particularly issues related to incest (*ruaal*) and homicide (*luy*) which were normal practices at the time. The original spelling of the term is "Nueer", meaning contamination or sins from which the term 'Nuer" was formed, replacing Naath gradually, until many people know only Nuer instead of Naath. It is an ethnic sense that the term Naath is used referring to the Nuer people found in South Sudan, who either use it positively or negatively as it was initially referred to Nueer (contamination or sin).

 It was a common practice among the Nuer /Naath people to marry close relatives as noted earlier in this chapter. There were rules and customs governing marriages among deferent tribes (communities) in ancient times, but it is not the intention of this text to explain these types of marriage contracts. However, it will be important to show how the Nuer abolished such practice of marrying a close relative when the Nuer elders agreed to enforce sanctions that would avert all those practices that do not conform to their cultural norms and values including: incest, theft, and murder. Under these new laws, it was agreed that if someone commits an incest or murder, there must be cleansing ceremony straightaway. For example, when the Nuer elders were developing these sanctions, they slaughtered a bull and split into two halves as a sign of separating the culprits involved in the incest to avoid its taboo and implications (Gatkuoth, 2022). Sharon Hutchinson explains this concept of incest sufficiently in her book the "Nuer Dilemma" published in 1996. According to Nuer oral traditions, it was from this point at *Kuer Kuong,* that the Nuer started marrying outside from their blood lines. It is worthy of note that there are social entitlements in the form of bride wealth distribution to relatives, that equally hinders incestuous practice (Gatkuoth, 2022). This practice of marrying a relative, however, remained with the Arabs after the floods and the subsequent destruction of Babel. Until now, Arabs marry cousins as their wives. Nuer/Naath, in contrast, have completely abolished that practice and performed some sacrifices to seal the covenant (*nguɔt*) between themselves as a community and between them and God. Similarly, in the case of homicide, if a Nuer kills another person, it should be reported immediately to the concerned spiritual leader (*Leopard Skin Chief*), who would perform rituals to avoid the blood of the victim haunting (*Nueer*) the murderer.

The Nuer (*Naath*) have undocumented myths from the ancient passed down to the current generations by the word of mouth through stories and songs. These myths give lenses that guide the Nuer to see beyond and make sanctions which help them understand and sustain their daily lives. The early culture of the Nuer (*Naath)* displays the patterns of behaviors that led to creation of myths that explain the Nuer origin toward their indigenous culture. There were strong links on observing the myths on how the Nuer were created centuries of their existence and the role of elders who read them and interpret their meanings to their children. The Nuer believe that they descended from heaven and gave birth to two clans that could be seen today in Nuer Nation. The second myths, relates to Nuer origin is the one pre dated *Koat Liech* in western Nuer which describe; that a man called GAW had three sons from whom other Nuer clans come from. The final myth is that of Jikäny Nuer whose grandfather *Kiir Kaker* is said to have been cut or brought out from a gourd that was flowing from the river. These tales describe Nuer origin actions during migration periods from south Kordufan, to western Nuer (Bentiu) and to the eastern Nuerland.

Nuer settlement and seasons
Throughout South Sudan's historical resistance to foreign invaders, the country's ethnic groups have continuously moved southward (South Sudan) where different ethnic communities, including the Nuer (*Naath*) settled. Nuer land occupies the swamps on both sides of the south Upper Nile, where they settled according to the lineage (*Kar marä*) system. Nuer were traditionally divided into three regional federations: The western Nuer residing west of Bhar el Jebel, the central of Zeraf Vavelly Nuer, the Eastern Nuer with Atwot excluded. The Atwot group have been historically part of the Nuer Homeland, but have moved towards the status of a separate cultural group (Kelly, 1985). Atwot were formerly a section of the Nuer occupying the present border between the Jagei and Dok Nuer. Nuer traditions hold that the Atwot migrated southward as a result of conflicts with other Nuer groups. However, Atwot migration and causes of their conflicts lie outside the scope of this text.

The Nuer people have four seasons in their calendar which include; *T̲ɔt* (summer), *Jiɔm* (winter), *Mäi* (spring) and *Ruel* (autumn). These seasons are associated with their environments such as drought, flood, hunger, and conflict. All of these have a direct impact on how the Nuer manage to live within such threatening conditions. They have twelve months in their calendar which divide the four seasons into two; "*t̲ɔt*" and "*Mäi*" which are known as wet and dry seasons and most Nuer adult can state them in order (see appendix 2). During each time of the year, certain social activities are prohibited for instant, in around January, February and March weddings are not allowed to take place in the past because the months are too hot and jeopardized newly wedded couples to enjoy their honeymoon. When the Nuer are approaching the dry season - hot months, each family offers sacrifices to the spirits (gods) to allow their families have peace and harmony during that period. During wet season (*t̲ɔt*) when they begin to plant their crops and there is too much rain that may spoil the crops, the Nuer turn to their spiritual experts who are assumed to have the powers to stop the rains or carry the clouds away and prevent it from raining. Those experts have the powers of the god of; wind and water and would always plead to them in such environments. The powers of these experts according to Nuer traditions, are usually noticeable from those whose relatives have mysteriously vanished as a result of wind or killed by a lightening which they called *Cholwic*. There are understandings that impacted the way Nuer give sacrifices and called the dead to respond on their crisis. In such situations, the relatives of *Cholwic* (deceased) call the dead person to assist them to stop the rain or any misfortune that may come to them.

The Nuer migrated seasonally to higher grounds during the wet season to avoid floods, and back to low grounds with plenty of water during the dry season. Because of the environment, the Nuer constantly moved between the cattle camps and their permanent villages in dry seasons. The Nuer movements were dictated by two seasons known as *"tɔt"* (the rainy season) and *"mäi"* (the dry season). Much of Nuer land is flooded during the rainy season between June and October. Towards December, the shift of villages begins, resources become scarce and most families migrate to the cattle camps. This seasonal migratory habit makes the Nuer a pastoralist community. During the seasonal migrations, the young men take cattle to the pasture. This type of movement among the Nuer is known as transhumance (*Yoth*) - movement of people, with their animals (mainly cattle) to new pastures which is quite distant from their home settlements. It is characterized by only a part of the community moving seasonally one place to another while the rest remain in the permanent villages. Usually, the section of the community that remains clear farms, build new huts and attend to any necessary repairing. These activities do not guarantee food security that is necessary for good nutrition in most of the Nuer occupied areas. As a result, transhumance has relegated the Nuer to nomadism. The Nuer villages are mainly made of strong, mud-walled, small-doored, windowless huts with, cylindrical grass roofs. The small doors force people to stoop down when entering houses. The nomadism of the community has been accentuated by the civil wars, most of which have been fought in or around Nuer habitations both in the colonial periods and after the independence of South Sudan. The proximity to war has made it difficult for the community to access quality life services like education, health and clean drinking water among such other services.

Traditions of the Nuer (*Naath*) People
While consulting international and regional cultures, the history of Nilotic peoples is dominated by a phenomenal migration process, settlement and expansion against their neighbours. As a result, the Nuer experienced widespread separation and cultural assimilation of other ethnic communities. Previous researchers such as Jal (2013) revealed that the Nuer along with other Nilotic groups settled along the Bahr el Gahzal and Sobat rivers in South Sudan around 14th century.

The Nuer people lived together in their homeland - Bentiu west of the River Nile until 18th century when they started to separate because of the conflicts among different sections. Also, Nuer migration was largely due to the impact of dramatic ecological and demographic problems which together had posed a threat to the natural productive resources. Feuds within the homestead triggered by a power struggle led to a split and subsequently, during their expeditions to the river of the east (*kiir känycäŋ*), assimilation of Nuer to other cultural groups and theirs to others started to emerge. These developments caused some Nuer to migrate out of Bentiu eastward, all the way into western borders of Ethiopia, displacing, observing and integrating many other ethnic communities into their culture.

The period after 1970s witnessed remarkable territorial expansion of the Nuer to Eastern River Nile (*kiir känycäŋ*). Consequently, Nuer expansion reached southeastern part of Ethiopia in the second half of the 19th century. It was one of the most famous mass movements in this century that has much historical commentary in the secondary anthropological literature (Johnson, 2016). During that period, various groups of Nuer crossed the Nile from their western homelands, forming new settlements in the east. A cluster of Jikäny Nuer, having been defeated by their western Dinka neighbors, took advantage of a civil war in the Shilluk Kingdom and passed through Shilluk territory into the Sobat valley (Jal, 1913; Stringham, 2016) and Jonson, 2016). The other groups that similarly benefited from the disruption caused by the entry of the Zariba system into the Sobat and Zaraf valleys moved into territories abandoned by their previous owners were the Lou Nuer and the Gawäär. The Zariba system encouraged commercial camps and defined the military – commercial attractiveness of slavaery in the 19th century in Sudan. The system introduced southern Sudan to a network of international credit that linked the camps of the traders to commercial companies' operatimg out of Khartoum -Sudan, Egypt and Europe. It was through Zariba system that southern Sudan was conquered pacified and governed (Johnson D.2016). Johnson further noted that the process of opportunistic settlement was not halted by the twentieth-century demarcation of a boundary between Sudan and Ethiopia. The environmental change and war both encouraged continued Nuer movement into Ethiopia from the twentieth into the twenty-first century (Johnson, 2016). The Nuer migration was more a settlement than a conquest, and the indigenous Dinka and Anyuak populations were as often rearranged as displaced persons. Assimilation into Nuer communities was achieved through adoption and intermarriage. And as time goes on Nuer age-set system, in which young men were initiated into adulthood enabled foreign men to marry Nuer women and fight alongside their Nuer age-mates (Stringham 2016; Johnson, 2016)). As a result of assimilation and the creeping expansion of Nuer settlements, kinship ties cut across Nuer lineages and tribal boundaries. Some Nuer communities had closer links with near foreign neighbors than with more distant Nuer sections, thus increasing the likelihood of inter-Nuer feuds when Nuer sections defended their Dinka or Anyuak kin against other Nuer raiders. By the beginning of the 20th century, Nuer, Dinka, and Anyuak communities lived interspersed and intermixed and Dinka language was still widely spoken throughout the Nuer settlements.

The Gaawäär were the first Nuer to begin crossing the Bahr el Jebel to the east in the early 18th century. Individual families who found that their pastures were inundated and that they could paddle across the unusually low Bahr el Jebel took up residence first in unoccupied parts of the river's east bank that until then had been submerged. Around the same time, other Nuer farther north started moving in the same direction, as population growth prompted an exodus (Stringham, 2016). The Lou confederation began to split up, with some remaining among the

Jagei confederation in western Nile (now Koch County), while others crossed the Bahr el Jebel, which is said to have been remarkably shallow. These Lɔu Nuer migrants, initially only a few colonists, rapidly grew to become their own confederation called the Lɔu which is now far larger than any other Nuer confederation. Soon afterward, the entire Thiäŋ and L_ak confederations also crossed over, which compelled the Lɔu and Gaawäär to keep moving farther east, where they began assimilating local Padaŋ. Finally, the Jikäny at the confluence of the Bahr el Ghazal and Bahr el Jebel also split up. As with the Lɔu, some Jikäny remained in their former territory in the west. Some of those who departed initially headed north toward Jebel Liri, the southern edge of the Nuba Mountains. However, prospects of success to the north soon darkened, and they then turned east and joined other Jikäny who in traversing *collo* country, crossed the White Nile, and settled between the Sobat and the Machar Marshes in 1828. This was the first account of Nuer migrations to the east of the Nile that still describes much of the historical background in anthropologies of "the Nuer" Stringham, (2016). This forms the settlement of the Nuer in the eastern banks of the River Nile from the 1820s to the 1850s.

Three Nuer great leaders emerged during this migration period: Bough Käpɛl (Gaawäär), Bidit (Lɔu) and Latjɔɔr Diŋyian (Jikäny), who during migration crossed the Nile in different points and periods. In their expeditions, they were intermarrying with the various ethnic communities they met, and assimilating their cultures into theirs as noted earlier, as they were migrating to Eastern Nile. The Nuer crossed the Nile to the east through three main points: Gaawäär *Pawarjak* (Fort), Lɔu Nuer crossed through *Wath Yokä* (Ford) and Jikäny crossed via *Wath ŋöök* (blue heron) crossing point. It is not the intention of this text to discuss the details of these expeditions. Some of these have been sufficiently detailed by Giet Jal, in his book *History of South Sudan's Jikäny Nuer Ethnic Group*. There are also other Nuer /Naath groups with similar culture who inhabited the Gambella Region in South Western part of Ethiopia as noted earlier. However, this is mentioned only in passing since this group is not a concern of the text's brief historical background of the Nuer Nation in South Sudan.

The Nuer original homeland – Bentiu - had experienced ecological changes and demographic problems at the beginning of the nineteenth century. These challenges forced the inhabitants to migrate from the Bahr el-Jebel to the east into the Zaraf Island. The Nuer homeland is located west of Bar el Jebel, between Lake Shambe in the Southeast and Lake "No", north of the vast swamps of the Sudd region, at the confluence of the Bahr el Jebel and Bahr el Ghazal Rivers (Jal, 2013). The Nuer were divided into two main groups; the Ɣ*ää*k and the Gëë. According to the Nuer traditional story, Ɣ*ää*k and Gëë are said to be brothers, through whom other Nuer clans attach themselves. Their father's name is *piny* (earth). He bequeathed his community a central homeland, *Koat Liech/ Jiath Liech*, a tamarind tree in present Jagei Nuer of Koch County in Unity State (Bentiu). This location is now a venue of certain ritual ceremonies and has become a shrine and holy place which in the western Nuer is called *därcheng* (center of home land). It is believed that the location is also the separation point of the two brothers - Ɣ*ää*k and Gëë. Ɣ*ää*k expanded southwards and Gëë northwards, established their holds and expanded against their neighbour's wishes.

The journey goes back to an ancient time, around the founding of the Nuer homeland *"Koat Liech"* currently, western Upper Nile, Unity State, in South Sudan. The Nuer people called themselves *''Naath''* plural form for all human beings (Jal, 2013, Kim, 2017, Riam, (2022) and Duany (1992). At the beginning of the nineteenth century all Nuer were living west of the Nile and by the end of that century the Nuer had moved and occupied an area stretching from the White Nile, north-east of the river Sobat and North-west of the Bahr el Ghazal, eastwards to the Ethiopian frontier, and southwards along the Pibor river to the borders of Murle country and across to Bahr el Zeraf. Howell (2018) observes five periods in Nuer migration history: first the period before they moved eastwards, about which little is known and might had been fewer in numbers, but more closely united as a group of people. Secondly, the period of initial invasion when they moved eastwards in a series of waves which began with cattle raids and ended in permanent occupation of other people's land mainly the Dinka and Anyuak ethnic communities. Thirdly, the period of numerical expansion by natural processes and by the absorption of huge numbers of Dinka and therefore adapted much of Dinka culture. This period was characterized by the facility with which Dinka elements were incorporated into Nuer society without resistance. The third period was followed immediately by a period of disharmony, suspicion, internal strife and political fission. The fourth period was the pressure from the north increased, a return to a semblance of cohesion was necessary and there emerged the great Nuer leaders led by 'traditional spiritual leaders' who arose as symbols of tribal resistance to foreign aggression. Finally, the period of British administration limited to an attempt to hold the Nuer from their attacks on their neighbours and to prevent fighting among the Nuer themselves and to the collection of taxes which the Nuer vigorously resented.

Between 1899 and 1930 there were thirty-six military patrols and campaigns against the Lɔu and Gaawäär Nuer in 1902, 1914, 1915, 1917, and 1927-30; and the eastern Jikäny Nuer in 1919-20; and the Western Nuer in 1923, 1925, and 1928. The last "pacification" campaign in all of British Africa took place in Southern Sudan against the Nuer in 1928-30. In only eight of the first thirty-two years of the condominium was there no significant armed confrontation between a southern Sudanese community and government forces. In addition to these major campaigns there were smaller patrols, armed marches, and police actions where tax was collected by force (Johnson, 2016). As noted earlier, it was because of this use of force that the British government faced most resistance from the Nuer. Although government orders for collection of taxes and construction of roads were not done from a sense of moral obligation, they were honoured because the Nuer were afraid of retaliation.

This was a challenging period in Nuer political history. Rebellions among the Nuer mainly, the Lɔu and the Gaawäär of the Upper Nile Province in 1927 and 1928 was in its climax. Captain Fergusson, the District Commissioner of Western Nuer was assassinated; the Lɔu Nuer led by Gwɛk Ngundɛŋ had shown open disobedience for some time previously and in that year to the Gaawäär Nuer led by Dual Diu inclined on the Dinka of Bor District and attacked the government positions at Duk Payuel. Reprisals then followed and took the form of a series of vigorous military operations which were known as the 'Nuer Settlement' (Howell, 2018). The colonial administration decided to deal with Nuer Prophets in concerted military operation designed to isolate the Prophets from their people therefore facilitating their death or capture.

The objective of Nuer settlement was to punish individuals' section or sections among the Gaawäär and Lou Nuer sections rather than as a show of force to an administered people (Johnson, 2016). The government sent troops throughout the Nuer country east of the Nile. A full-scale settlement in 1929, aimed at concentrating the Lou Gaawäär in specified areas where they would be isolated from their Dinka neighbours and other groups of Nuer. The Prophets were rooted out of their hiding places, and once military operations had been successfully completed, a vigorous new attempt to administer the Nuer would begin, with force labour - building of roads, dispensaries and administrative centers and the organisation of the Nuer into a new administrative system under government appointed chiefs was realized. It was after this retaliation that the feelings of fear and suspicion in those situations were eradicated and the foundation of the sound administrative structure was started and the Nuer rapidly adopted themselves to these new arrangements.

Along with their neighboring Dinka, the Nuer formed the sub-division of the largest East African cultural groups known as the Nilotes, which also includes: the Luo, Shilluk and Anyuak who called themselves Collo and Anywaa, respectively. The linguistic similarities, physical appearances and customs between these groups contain a shared vocabulary indicated resulting from a common origin and mutual influence, eliminating any doubt about their common origins though the history of their divergence is unknown. It is certain that the Nuer and the Dinka have a common "origin", and archaeological research indicates that the spread of domesticated animals in this region of African continent was concurrent with the origin of distinct ethnic identities.

Roots of Nilotes

The relationship between Nilotic people in South Sudan extends to the whole continent of Africa. Among the Luo ethnic groups in then Sudan, there is a common belief that all of their groups are part of a larger ethnic family, which is comprised of all the Luo in Sudan, Kenya, Uganda, Tanzania, Democratic Republic of the Congo, and Ethiopia. The narrative of migration and origin, and the myth of common ancestreal African roots is shared by the Luo groups in South Sudan. In South Sudan, the Shilluk and the Anyuak are found in the Upper Nile region; Acholi and Jo-Pariri in the Equatoria region; and Jo-Luo, Thurri and Bor in the Eastern and Western Bahr el Ghazal region (Madut, 2020). Although this relationship limits itself to three South Sudanese ethnic communities and the Luo of Kenya in this text, first it gives a general overview of common features among Black African people; sharing of names of clan and places. The mythical hero of the Shilluk is called Nyikang which is merely a variant of the clan name Nyang so widespread among the Nuer. The Dengkak (*Jäŋ*) people lived in cooperation with the Nuer and the Shilluk. This shows that a relationship exists between the Dinka in South Sudan and the Nyang of Senegal. The Wolof were from legendary order of the Lak (Nuer) and claimed to have been excluded legendary order of the Lak, the allusion being an order of knighthood of bygone days which did not take questions of honour lightly. Although, no Wolof was able to say when or where this Lak community existed. It was therefore assumed to connect it with the Nuer tribe of the Lak (clan) who were described as warlike people knightly traditions justify the legends current in Wolof society. The Lak tribe (Nuer) of the Upper Nile are not the same with the Laka tribe among the Sara, situated on the Wolofs hypothetical migration route. The Wolof word *lakâ* (means foreign, which speak a language other than Wolof, that sum up and reflect this historical relations with the Nuer. The Nuer clan of the Gaanwar (gawäär) brings to mind the Gelwar (Serer or Mandingo) of Senegal: Dar tut (Nuer personal proper name). *Tut* - the Bull, the ancestor. Diop (1978), captures this commonalities as highlighted here: In Ancient Egyptian epoch, *Tut* refers to the miniature portrait statuette of the deceased or the ancestor. In Wolof *tut* means 'small'. Hence the name of the Ndar Tut quarter in Saint-Louis, Senegal, could well have quite a different and remote origin from that ascribed to it by most people or by popular etymology. Dar also, is a very common name among the Nuer, where Tut Nyang and similar words befall. There are other complex proper names also found in Senegal such as gɔl (hot ash fire (Nuer)); *gel* (hot ash fire (Wolof)), *Jit (jiith* (scorpion (Nuer)); *Jit* (scorpion (Wolof)) and so on. But the Nuer language differs from Wolof in structure and vocabulary. This brings us to the attention of the Anu, a black race which peopled Egypt in early historical times; often represented in early Egyptian texts. According to Diop (1978), Black people called Anu came from Great Lakes region and Southern Africa, populated Egypt from South to North. They settled first between the Sudan and southern Egypt and went down the Nile and conquered the entire country. The civilization that was in Egypt had its roots from the Great Lakes and Southern Africa where humans were born and remains were traced, and this is why ancient Egyptians designated Great Lakes and Southern Africa as the Holy Land of the gods. Before any records were written, sources suggest that the group that came to be known as 'Nilotic' migrated from the Great Lakes region, nearer to the source of River Nile (Diop, 1978).

In the same area of the Upper Nile were the Anyuak tribe still found. The Anyuak are descended from Gile, second brother of Nyikang, the mythical ancestor of the Shilluk (Collo). Guile is a Senegalese place-name made famous by the Battle of Guile (at the foot of the tamarind tree in Guile) between the Kayor and the Djoloff, supposedly the furthest point reached by the Shilluk, Dieng and Nyang (Nuer) tribes of the Nile. The Berri live around Mount Lépoul (Upper Nile) and must not be confused with the Beir or the Bari. Bari is a Fulani name, while Beir is the typical local name for Gorée Island. The Jaluo, Jalloh (Jallo is a Senegalese Fulani name) and Gaya (Gaye, Senegal) live on the banks of Lake Victoria. The Ndau and the Sena (Serer names in Senegal) live side by side south of the Zambesi near the shores of the Indian Ocean. The Ciec or Seek live among the Dieng or Dinka. The Pual or Pul are Nuer. The Kombolle and the Pelel are Nyaro matrileneal clans. The Luo (Lo in Senegal and northern Ivory Coast) are Nuer living in Dieng (Dinka) territory east of the Nile (Diop, 1978). They were found side by side in closeness such as Senegalese towns bearing in mind the role for the founding of settlements according to which they were usually named after their founders. This brief description gives us a hint on how black people were closely related in culture, language and names in those days; from which the relationship between the Nuer and other ethnic groups can be drawn.

This chapter discusses the relationship between the Nuer and other ethnic groups. Some of these relations are presumed and told orally or myths without real backing. The Nuer use their knowledge, practices concerning nature and the universe: applying know-how and skills that they have developed by interacting with their natural environments, which they expressed through language, memories, spirituality or worldviews. Others are historical facts cemented with sources. I begin with Nuer perspective of Luo of Kenya relations. This is because, the Nuer/Naath are said to have been a section of the "Naath People "that migrated out of Gizera into a desert land which they then called *"Kuer Kuoŋ"*, located in southern Kordofan as noted earlier in chapter one, that after centuries of isolation and influence from Luo peoples triggered them to be a distinct ethnic group from Naath. And partly because the Luo of Kenya are said to have started their migration from South Sudan which some Nuer elders claimed was Bentiu, the "Nuer homeland", after Luo three groups got parted: *Nyikang, Dimo* and *Gilo*, because of the quarrel among them, triggered by a power struggle in the year 1300 in Eastern Bahr el Ghazal that led to a split and subsequently, separating as a nation, into different subgroups and going into different directions (Ojijo, 2012). The Kenyan Luo migrated to Kenya through Uganda, using the western Bank of the Nile River where the Nuer first settled.

Nuer - Luo relations

The Luo in Kenya: Kenya is a country in Eastern Africa, which borders the Indian Ocean between Somalia and Tanzania. It covers an area of about 582,650 sq.km; with a population of 33,829,590 and about 3,185,000 are members of the Luo ethnic group (Madut 2020). The Kenyan Luo assume that South Sudan is their central point of migration and their home of origin.

Nuer–Luo relations can be traced back to the period of massive migrations of (tribes) different ethnic communities from Egypt to South Sudan where many of the Nilotes settled. As we noted above, the Naath community Nuer was a section of the "Naath People" that migrated out of Gizera into a desert land ("*Kuer Kuong*") and that the influence from Luo people caused the Nuer to be a distinct ethnic group from Naath. This could justify Nuer oral interpretation that needs to be explained. The Nuer claimed that when they were in their homeland - Bentiu, a man named Gaw Ran is said to be the father of, Gëë and Kuoh, through whom other Nuer clans attach themselves except Kuoh who had been reported to have migrated southwards when they were still in Bentiu leaving behind his two brothers: Ɣääk and Gëë some of whom later migrated to what they then called "*kiir Känychäŋ*" (river of the east) east of the Nile where they finally settled. Folklore source states that Kuoh decedants are now Luo community found in Kenya, some of whom are also said to have settled in Alliab area and now Dinka Alliab in Warrab State; who still fairly speak both Dinka and Nuer languages as situation demands.

 Historically, the Luo were one of many tribes (communities) of people resident at a settlement known as Napata, Upper Egypt (Northern Sudan) between 5500 BC and 3500 BC, during these periods of migration from Egypt, through Kush, Meroe, and Aksum to Sudan. The communities were controlled by the Nubians under one of the first sacral kingdoms to arise in the Nile, Ta-Seti, located in northern Nubia. Around 3200 BCE, there was further consolidation of the sacral kingdoms. These people were black, Negroes, and the Luo were part of these groups of people.

South Sudan is hence the first place where the Luo were called *Jo Luo*; and subsequently, it is the birth place of the Luo Nation as a distinct group of people. The Luo got their name in Sudan in the 10th century and this is why most tales of the origin of the Luo nation start from South Sudan; at *Dog nam,* the Acholi equivalent of *dhonam*, which is *DhoLuo* for *"Mouth of the Lake"*— that is a *lakeshore*. Whereas there is no agreement on which lake it is most historians identify it as Lake No or The three are the same thing (Ojijo, 2012). The Luo groups (*Nyikang, Dimo* and Gilo) lived together in Eastern Bahr el Ghazal before they were separated in the year 1300. As mentioned earlier, that there were feuds within their homestead triggered by a power struggle that led to a split and consequently, separate history of the three groups. It was also during this period that Luo started separating as a nation into different sub groups and going into different directions, while also intermarrying with the various groups they met, and assimilating their cultures, or being assimilated into other cultures. Luo share cultures with other communities they met earlier in Egypt, Kush, Meroe and Aksum, and for this reason the Luo culture is seen across 16 language groups in 13 countries including Sudan, where the Nuer original land - Bentiu is located. It was therefore possible during that Nuer – Luo acquaintances might have been cordial and this could mean naming Kuoh (Luo) speaking group a brother to Ɣ*ää*k and Gɛ̈ɛ̈, who are from Nilotes speaking cluster.

Luo speaking group still have similarities with the Nilotic group such as the Nuer having similar culture, like sharing of names, for example, *piu* (water) *wang* (eye), *kuän* (*kuon*) among other possessions. Moreover, the sub-division of East African cultural groups known as Nilotes, includes the Luo, Shilluk and Anyuak, Dinka and the Nuer whose lineage might have been one from which the Luo migrated further to Kenya when they emigrated from northern Khartoum to Wau, Bahr el Ghazal in South Sudan, where they interacted with Jur Chol. From 990 to 1125 the Luo were still in Sudan, at Wau, Bahr el Ghazal; after which, a serious outbreak of anthrax *(Nyapec)* and population explosion whipped out their livestock. Following this incident, the community resorted to fishing along the River Nile for survival, and this is how the Luo earned the names *Jo-oluo-Aora (*people who follow the river) and later some Luo migrated into Kenya through eastern Uganda, arriving sometime around 1500 AD at different intervals (Ojijo, 2012).

It is not the intension of this text to give a full detail history of how and why Kuoh decided to leave his motherland, but just only to mention how the two brothers Ɣ*ää*k and Gɛ̈ɛ̈, departed with their brother Kuoh and where he might have gone and now could be traced. Whether this Nuer narrative of Kuoh (Luo) as a brother to Ɣ*ää*k and Gɛ̈ɛ̈ is true or not, some Nuer elders perceived it as a historical fact that may require further research on how Luo is related to Nilotic speaking groups in particular, the Nuer people of South Sudan.

Nuer - Shilluk interaction
The Luo Shilluk/Collo: are the descendants of the great Luo ancestor, Nyikang, who was the first founder of the Luo kingdom in Africa. Most Luo oral histories and myths acknowledge Nyikang to be the second son, who caused disunity, disintegration and family breakdown within the greater Luo ethnic group in Sudan before their migration into other parts of Africa. Their disputes later led to further displacements and migrations both internally within South Sudan and externally to the neighboring African countries such as Congo, Uganda, Kenya, Ethiopia and Tanzania (Madut 2020). After the dispute between Nyikang and his brother Dimo, Nyikang managed to create the first Luo kingdom in the Upper Nile region in Southern Sudan due to his charismatic leadership style. Collo kingdom has been sustained by Nyikang's descendants to the present day. Kings in Luo Shilluk are traditionally known as Reth are selected according to bloodline. The Shilluk link their first ancestral origins before the kingdom to the great father Dhyang aduk, who was followed by Omaro wad Dhang aduk, Kolo wad Omaro, Moul wad Kolo, and Okwa wad Moul. The Collo Kingdom, existed from 1590 to 1992, it was ruled by 34 kings during this period (Madut, 2020).

Nyikang was the father of Shilluk (Collo) nation, who moved northward along the Nile to re-conquer and settled the land their ancestors had lost to the Arabs and Europeans. His son Dak was the most influential in the establishment of the kingdom. The Collo is a nation with a common territory, a common language, a central authority to which all citizens pay allegiance, have an elaborate system of customs and traditions which inform on the attitudes of the people, the exercise of power and all other social relations.

The Collo community prefers to be known as Collo rather than the more widely known term, Shilluk and their language as dhok-Collo. The Collo, are a major Luo ethnic group of South Sudan, who occupies the land between the River Nile and the fringes of the Kordofan Province, from latitude 11 in the north to about 80 miles west of Tonga, as well as the east bank of the River Nile around the Sobat River junction for about 20 miles. The Shilluk are classified as Nilo-Saharan, Eastern Sudanic and Nilotic. The Collo are known as the most organized people, having a divine king which symbolizes the whole monarchy in their kingdom. Their kingdom is divided into north (gar) and south (lwak). The capital of the Collo kingdom is Pachodo. The major towns are Malakal (Makal), Kodhok (Kal Doro), Tonga (Tungu) and Wad Akon (Ojijo, 2012).

Nuer–Shilluk relations started during Nuer difficult expedition period to the east of the Nile from which their first social engagement in form of marriage made the two ethnic communities aided the other. Jal (2013) narrates their first engagement: Latjɔɔr Duach leader of Jikäny Nuer presented a beautiful girl, daughter of a man called Riar Yak from the Wangkeach section and a number of gifts, to the Shilluk Reth Awin. In their meeting, gifts were exchanged and a young girl named Nyajiech Riei was offered to the Shilluk Reth Awin as a wife in return for safe passage through the Shilluk land. In the meantime, the Nuer migrants were requested by the Reth to assist him in putting down the Shilluk (Collo) Civil war that subsequently led to the defeat of the Shilluk rebel nyireth (*prince*) Otor Akol of Pabur, in favour of Reth Awin. Nuer–Shilluk relations continued and remain well-mannered in many aspects including; better understanding among their traditional and political leaders which added to the already existed social developments built over many years.

The Nuer–Anywaa connection
The Anyuak (Anywaa) are the second largest Luo subgroup in the Upper Nile region - South Sudan. Gilo was the Anyuak Luo group's great ancestor and the founder of Annyuak Kingdom in Upper Nile, Region. The Anyuak live across the Ethiopian and South Sudanese border. The Annyuak groups in Ethiopia are found in the Gambella region of south western Ethiopia and both groups in Ethiopia and South Sudan do not officially recognize the borders imposed by the colonial powers, and continue to celebrate their common sociocultural and ethnic norms and traditions in both countries. Hence, inciting conflicts with their neighbours. The concept of political boundaries has caused considerable legal and national loyalty issues within these Luo subgroups. The Anyuak are descendants of Gilo, the youngest brother of Nyikang and Dimo, who are regarded as the Luo's great ancestors; Nyikang and Dimo migrated from Bahr el Ghazal to the Upper Nile region. The Anyuak are found in Pibor's Adminstrative Area and Akobo County in Jonglei state. Like their cousins collo, the Anyuak are classified as Nilo-Saharan, Eastern Sudanic and Nilotics.

The Nuer interaction with the Anyuak goes back to the 18th century and had not been cordial. In the process of Nuer expansion, they forced the Anyuak to migrate further east into Ethiopia and incorporated many of their community members. Jal (2013), noted that when the Nuer arrived on the Sobat (east of the Nile), they found the Anyuak in possession of the land immediately along the banks of the Sobat, from Abuong in the west to the mouth of the Khor Jokau in the upper reaches of the Sobat in the east, the whole of Wanding along the Pibor and Adura Island in the triangle country. The first initial Nuer advances against the Anyuak, took place around the first decade of the second half of the nineteenth century (Jal, 2013). Further east, the Jikany had begun raiding the Anyuak on the Bongjak (Oboth) River by 1855, and on the Baro by 1860 the Eastern Jikäny also appear to have been well established in the general area of their present territory. However, substantial pockets of Dinka and Anyuak settlements persisted along the Sobat for many years after this period. Many of these settlements gradually disappeared through assimilation rather than expulsion and this process played an important role in the consolidation of Jikany territorial gains. In addition, Akobo County which is now settled by both MOR Lɔu Nuer and Annyuak was originally a territory of Anyuak (Anywaa). In about the end of the 1860s, the Nuer–Annyuak Agreement was reached stopping Nuer hostilities in eastern Jikäny. Eventually, Nuer–Anyuak relations started to improve (Jal, 2013). The two communities had then intermarried specially, the eastern Jikäny and Mor Lɔu Nuer. Most of the Annyuak found in Upper Nile region in Southern Sudan had been assimilated into Nuer culture mainly those who lived in eastern Jikäny as noted above.

About 1870, The Lɔu and Jikäny Nuer conducted a combined raids against the Anyuak to the east had gradually made the Anyuak withdraw further up the tributaries of Sobat river to the upland region the Nuer currently occupy. The Nuer advanced along the Akobo and Oboth where they, destroyed most of the villages, including the populous village of Ukaadi, as far as the sacred rock' Abula, near ubaa village at the southeastern extremity of Anyuak land. Both the Lɔu and Jikäny, came with their families with intention to settle in Anyuak land. The invasion seriously broke up the Anyuak. Many were killed and many died in the famine that resulted, though it was mitigated by the stores of milled they had hidden in deep holes in the ground before fleeing into the bush. Most of their cattle were stolen. The Lɔu and eastern Jikäny launched a massive invasion of upland Anyuak territory that penetrated to its extreme southeast border during the same decade. Although the Nuer had intended to settle in the areas along the Akobo and Oboth from which they evicted the Anyuak. They withdrew rapidly after trypanosomiasis reduced their herds. The Lɔu Nuer made no further efforts to appropriate up land Anyuak territory afterward (Raymond, 1985).

Towards the end of the nineteenth century, the Anyuak acquired a large number of rifles from various Ethiopian sources in exchange for ivory and to use these guns to hunt elephants and procure additional ivory. Opportune with these, the Anyuak added to their tools for defense. By 1911, the Anyuak had their possession twenty-five thousand rifles as against one thousand held by the eastern Jikany, who had more limited contact with some of the same sources. Possession of firearms enabled Anyuak to enlarge the number of villages over which they exercised political control, and this increased the fighting force they were able to mobilize against the Nuer (Pritchard, 1940). The Annyuak have been the victims of Nuer raids, took the offensive twice during this period: Armed expeditions sent against the Jikany, but both were beaten back. In June 1911 the Anyuak carried out a successful attack against Lɔu Nuer settlements, capturing a number of women and cattle. The Nuer mobilized a large force and succeeded in recovering these losses, but thirty-five Nuer were killed in the initial Anyuak raid and Nuer counterattack that followed. A second Anyuak raid on Lɔu community followed shortly. Thirty Nuer were killed, many women and children captured, and 240 head of cattle raided. In August, the Lɔu lost an additional five persons killed and 'unknown number 'of women and children and 150 head of cattle. In September raid the same year, twenty Nuer were killed and additional captives and 150 heads of cattle. By October, the Anyuak were reported to have established a base in Lɔu from which they extended their raids as far as Awoi in the middle of Gaawäär territory, killing a large number of Nuer men, capturing many women and cattle. The Anyuak force, led by Akweiwa Cam, consisted of four hundred well-armed men. At this point a gunboat was dispatched up the Sobat and Pibor Rivers. Anyuak settlements on the Pibor were shelled, causing considerable loss of life, and all accessible villages on the lower Akobo River were burned. In March of the following year (1912), a punitive expedition was carried out against the Anyuak noble (Akweiwa-cam) and his followers who were actually responsible for the earlier raids on the Nuer. Akweiwa-wa-cam's district was located on the upper Akobo, well beyond the limits of navigation that had restricted and defined the earlier gunboat expedition. Ninety Anyuak were reported killed and a number of villages burned by the British-led Sudanese army column. But the government force that consisted of 439 men likewise suffered heavy casualties; 47 killed and 12 wounded during the same year (Raymond, 1985).

The Jikäny and Lɔu Nuer undertook their own reprisal against the Anyuak. Directed against the Anyuak villages on the north bank of the Baro River from the Ethiopian border to Itang, they lived a distance of about fifty miles. Reports indicated' all the villages have been devastated and their cultivations destroyed. This raid demonstrates the Nuer capability to mount a large-scale counter offensive after experiencing a series of defeats. The key to this effectiveness in this respect was Nuer ability to comprise their internal differences and unite in the face of external aggression. In this context the Nuer set aside their long-standing feuds in order to combine against the Annyuak. This is one of the principal features of Nuer segmentary lineage organization which Pritchard (1940) referred to Nuer- Annyuak raiding tapered off in 1913 and 1914 and virtually ceased after 1915 (Kelly, 1985). The Nuer believe in right of possession of tools of war that they can use against any discriminating forces, whether union or associations, they act without patience to protect themselves from those who are longing to harm them (:(see Figure no 1). Ihere were five engagements during this period, which were quite minor points, the cessation of raiding to a strong government presence at the Akobo post; first established only in 1911 as part of the punitive action against the Annyuak.

In recent years however, relations between Lɔu Nuer and Annyuak deteriorated in Akobo County of Jonglei State resulting in loss of lives and properties. This is because of land issues and disputes over political representation and employment claimed by Annyuak community against their counterpart – the Mor Lɔu Nuer. Although, there has been no realistic justification on these claims, conflict happened anyway. Many Annyuak people left Akobo town and migrated to Ethiopia. Nonetheless, efforts are being made to restore harmony and peaceful co-existence between the two ethnic communities.

Let me put aside the sequence of Nuer- Annyuak and take up this Nuer- Dinka relations, as it forms the backdrop for their large-scale counter raids that resulted to a punitive expedition carried out against the Nuer nobles (Guɛk Ngundɛŋ and Dual Diu) in eastern Nuer, after which the colonial government established laws and regulations to hold those responsible for the earlier raids on the either side.

1.1 lineup strategy

1.2: taking defence positions

1.3: Combat

1.4: Some tools for war; *Tiop, With, Kot and Mut*

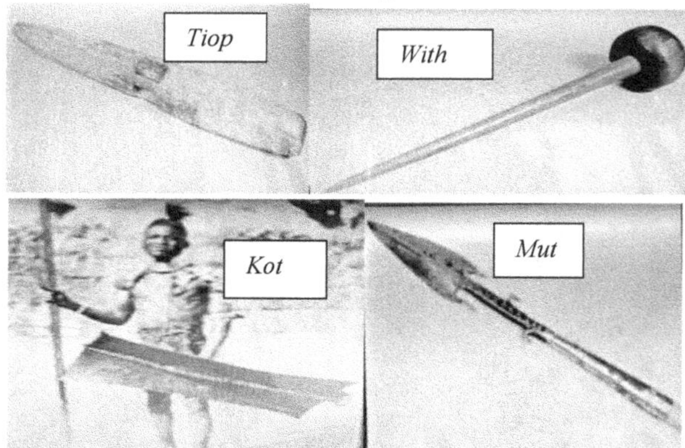

Collected & organized by the Author

Nuer-Dinka relations

Dinka (*Jieng*) people live in Savanna Region surrounding the central swamps of the Nile basin in South Sudan. They speak a Nilotic language classified within the Eastern Sudanic branch of the Nilo–Sharan languages and are closely related to the Nuer in history and culture. The beginning of the Nuer migration explains the Nuer–Dinka relationship which commenced sometime between 1817 and 1826. Oral folklore pertaining to the migration has been recorded by different authors such as Jal, 2013; Johnson, 1980 and Kelly 1985. Their assertions are largely consistent with respect to the main features of their direction. Firstly, Jikäny advanced to Jebel Liri on the edge of Nuba territory and then along the border area between the Nuba and the Shilluk. They then passed through Shilluk territory in the vicinity of Melut and crossed the Nile into Dinka territory, met with fighting, where they raided many of Dinka cattle and pushed the Dongjol Dinka North West. The Jikäny then turned south and proceeded to the lower Sobat River where they settled. As noted above, Jikäny migration began before 1817 and had already moved up the Sobat beyond Abuong by 1826. By 1860 they conquered an area that extended from the high ground in the north central part of what is presently Lɔu Nuer territory in the west to the foothills of the Ethiopian escarpment in the east (Kelly, 1985).

The Gaawäär formerly resided in the southern portion of Dok Nuer territory. They then crossed Bhar el Jebel and settled on the edge of the swamp near the slope of Zeraf Island (Pritchard.1940, Howell 1954, Kelly 1985) The Lɔu, originally occupied the southern part of Jagei territory crossed Bhar el Jabel about sometime -1820 extending their conquest through raiding. Making the Ngok Dinka who held the northern half of Zeraf Island withdrew under the pressure of the Lɔu raids and migrated into two separate groups; westward to the Bhar el Arab and eastward to the area between the Khor Fullus and the Sobat River. Similarly, the Gaawäär pushed the eastern Luach Dinka out of the southern half of Zeraf Island and the latter settled on the Khor Fullus opposite the eastern Ngok. This expulsion of the Dinka from Zaraf Island was completed by 1840s. This time Gaawäär already in possession of the high ground on the east banks of the Zeraf and ten years later they had advanced as far as Luang Deng (Luak Deng) by 1865 describes by Johnson (2016) as ("The Mecca of Nuer and Dinka" that contained the shrine of their deity (Deng Dit), (Johnson, 2016). About 1870, the Lɔu focused their attention to the Nyarraweng Dinka in the south. At about 1880, they sporadically settled eastern half of Nyarraweng territory which was largely controlled by the Lɔu while the eastern Jikäny attacked the Burun to the northeast. The Burun were still outside the sphere of British administrative attention and were raided without interference.

The intensity of Jikäny raids on the Burun later became apparent when colonial administration began to be extended into this area and reporting improved. There were seven Nuer raids in 1919 and four in 1920 before organized bombing of Jikäny settlements by the royal air force ended the Jikäny attacks. By 1880, Nuer territorial expansion was mostly completed. The Gaawäär made substantial gains in the occupation of the northern part of the ridge between 1878 and 1883 and the Lɔu evicted the Dinka from the southern part between 1885 and 1895. Generally, the swiftness of Nuer expansion started to slow considerably in the early 1880s and had nearly stopped by the early 1890s (Kelly, 1985), thus, harmonizing the relations between the two ethnic communities which their traditions claimed to have been genetically brothers.

Oral history tells us more about the relations of these two ethnic communities. The Dinka and the Nuer were said to be brothers of the same father, according to mythical tales. Dinka was the elder son, and the Nuer was the younger son. When their father grew old and became blind he had to divide the only old cow and calf to his sons. It was related that the old man for his own reasons liked Nuer- his younger son who he called one night to inform his intentions to offer him the calf at dawn. Meanwhile their mother who liked Dinka was patiently listening and told Dinka the conspiracy and advised him to go to his father at dawn and disguised himself as (Nuäär) Nuer. He did so. In the following morning of the actual inheritance, Dinka came first and when asked by their old blind father to identify himself, he pretended to be a Nuer and acquired the calf and walked away with it. When Nuer came later on, his father asked the same question upon which he responded, "I am Nuer." The father was annoyed with Dinka for his deception. He instructed Nuer to take the old cow but told him to follow Dinka to claim back the calf. It is assumed that this confusion begot the unending conflict between the two brothers and their ensuing communities. However, there is no source backing this mythical claim and where this incident took place. Though, both communities (Dinka and the Nuer) consider this tale as historical fact. It is certain that the Nuer and Dinka have a common "origin", and archaeological research indicates that the spread of domesticated cattle in South Sudan was contemporaneous with the origin of distinct ethnic identities, especially active period of Nuer eastward migration that began in the middle of the 19th Century. British colonial policy in Nuer land was aimed at setting boundary between the Nuer and Dinka, thus, effectively halting a dynamic process of cultural change that had been unfolding for centuries. Despite the constant conflicts caused by migration, the Nuer and Dinka remain neighbours who maintain unending contact, inter-marriage and adopt each other's cultural practices.

The Nuer's affirmation in this belief is cemented by Prophet Ngudɛŋ's prophesies and songs. One of his songs, loosely translated to "those Jieng outside will bring back my calf", "*ken Jääng raar badou yangdä noong ram pal täth ci ku goa*", is one such assertion. Although the song is not specific about the inheritance myth, the word *calf* in the lyrics is assumed to support the folklore. Ngundɛŋ Bong is a renowned Nuer Prophet who lived between c.1830 and 1906. His father Bong Chan was a "*kuär muon*" (earth master or leopard-skin chief), originally from the Bul Nuer in western Upper Nile (Bentiu). He emigrated to live among the *gaajiok* Nuer in the east. According to Johnson, Ngundɛŋ was initiated into the *Thut* age-set between 1855 and 1860s. He was possessed by *kuoth* (the god or divinity, specifically, *deng*). He prophesized many social and political changes, which the Nuer and other South Sudanese believe are happening now. Besides, he constructed a huge pyramid (*Bieh*) at Weideng, some few miles north of Waat Payam Nyirol County of Jonglei state, which attracted many visitors from Nuer, Dinka, Anyuak and others. In the latter half of the nineteenth century, Prophet Ngundɛŋ attempted to formulate a philosophy of social harmony within this mixed population that not only condemned Nuer inter-sectional feuds but prohibited raids against non-Nuer neighbors.

While ultimately unsuccessful in his lifetime, Ngundɛŋ's teachings took on a new meaning and acquired a greater audience in the 20th and 21st centuries as the Nuer became increasingly integrated into the wider South Sudanese society (Johnson, 1994). Throughout his life, Prophet Ngundɛng established a reputation for having the power of life and death. He was speaking with voice of *dɛng* through his songs and prayers. He enunciated a social philosophy of peace, condemned inter-Nuer feuds and raids against Nuer's neighbours.

Among the Ngundɛŋ's objects used in his rites included; a brass pipe (*töny lääng*), made by *Wäärjoguöl*, an *Anyuak* blacksmith, whom he recognized in his song as believer of *dɛng* (spirit) and *dang*, a ceremonial stick (translated by Johnson as a baton) but known as a rod among the scripturally-minded Nuer). The *dang* was fashioned from the root of a '*koat*'tarmarind tree. It measured about a meter long, and decorated with copper wire. The rod was broken at the battle of Padding in c.1879; the only battle reported where Ngundɛŋ fought in self-defense (Johnson, 2009) After *Ngundɛng's* death, his son *Guek* claimed he possessed the same spirit "*dɛŋ*". As a result, he inherited his father's relics, including; the pipe (*tony*) and the rod (*dang*). The rod was broken at the battle of Padding in 1879; the only battle reported where Ngundɛŋ fought in self-defense (Johnson, 2009). I was the first Nuer who knew when the rod was found and bought by Douglas Johnson in auction in 2000 after many years of its disappearance when it was taken by Priecy Corriat (*Gierkuac/Wang Yom*) in 1928. Douglas and I have a long friendship relations since 1975, when I was his personal assistant during his research field work on Nuer Prophets. When Douglas purchased the relics he wrote to me straight-away, we met and coordinated the return of *dang* to Sudan but because of the war (1983-2005), we decided and agreed to keep the rod in UK until peace is returned for its safety and also to avoid confusion and conflicts of interests. It was eventually returned to South Sudan in 2012 after having consultations with Douglas in his resident in Oxford United Kingdom together with Hon. Hussein Mar Nyuot and we requested him for the return of the dang. It had a huge community reception with eagerness in Juba international airport headed by Dr. Riek Machar Teny, who later kept the *dang* with him (s (see Figure no: 2.1 .2 & 2.3 below).

Figure 2: Ngundɛŋ's objects:

2.1: Rod (*dang*) & *Tony*.

Collected & organized by the author

From left: Prof. Douglas H. Johson, Hon. Hussein Mar Nyuot, Dr. Gabriel Gai Riam (author) & Philip Lyon Rousell (*Kerbiel*)

2.3: The reception of *dang* at Juba International Airport 2012.

Collected & organized by the author

It's to be recalled that after Ngundɛŋ's death, his son *Guɛk* claimed he was possessed by the same spirit *"dɛng"*. Guɛk's rise to prominence coincided with the British and Egyptian reign over Sudan. He was attacked by the British Royal forces and was killed on February 8, 1929, at Ngundɛŋ's pyramid (*Weidɛŋ)* Waat Payam - Nyirol County, Jonglei state - South Sudan.

The Anglo-Egyptian Condominium established the necessary Laws and regulations which were carefully considered and issued as required. The task before them however, also included building confidence of the people, to develop their resources (Kitchener, 1900). Initially, the Nuer together with their Nilotic neighbours resisted incorporation into the Sudanese political structure. This resistance led to the development of two distinct parts of the country: the North and South. As a result, a policy initiated by colonial administration in the 1930[s] called the closed districts divided the Sudan into two administrative areas. North Sudanese were self-identified as Arabs and Muslims while the South Sudanese including the Nuer identified themselves as black Africans and predominantly Christians and traditional believers. The classic description of the Nuer society is one that has been read by generation's anthropology such as Prof. Evans-Pritchard's studies of the Nuer in southern Sudan.

CHAPTER THREE:
SOCIAL SET UP

Segmentary Lineage (*Kaar maarä*)

Generally, the Nuer social set up presents them as people with a common ancestral descent sharing a close-knit tie of kinship and a common blood relationship. Such a group can claim exclusive rights to clan and lineage's property, between their members, by the rule of exogamy (marriage outside the family line). These links cement the Nuer into larger communities and societies, each possessing its own sense of common ethnic and cultural belonging.

Researchers show that the Nuer clan is not an undifferentiated group of people recognizing their common kinship compared to other Nilotic communities in South Sudan. However, they remain highly segmented. These societal segments are hereditary structures referred to as lineages (*kar maarä*). One of the fascinating characteristics of lineage among the Nuer is that they are aggregated upward into much larger lineages by tracing descent back to an earlier ancestor. As Fukuyama (2012) observed, the Nuer are well-developed and good example of segmentary lineage organization, where genealogical rules precisely determine social structure and status (Fukuyama, 2012). Considering that the Nuer are almost wholly exogamous, the lineages trace their descent to a common ancestor. The key characteristic of a lineage is that the relationship between members is traceable in genealogical terms (Fortes and Pritchard, 1966). The Nuer are split into segments: the largest segments being main sections which are further segmented into small sections and further into tertiary tribal sections that comprise a number of village communities which are composed of kinships and local groups. Nuer lineages fight with one another constantly, usually involving conflicts over cattle and girls issues, particularly elopement of young girls, which are central to their culture. Lineages fight with other lineages at the same level. But the Nuer can combine to fight external foes such as the Dinka, Murle and Anyuak and put aside their internal differences when such disputes arise. Nuer themselves state this structural principle clearly in the expression of their political values. They are a particularly well-developed and pure example of segmentary lineage organization, where genealogical rules precisely determine social structure and status (Fukuyama, 2012).

In most Nilotic societies in South Sudan, lineages are described as localized communities, where members have an association with localities and speak their local languages. In certain instances, the societies act as though they are an exclusive agnatic group. Every Nilotic village is associated with a lineage, and though its members comprise of a small proportion of the community, it is identified with them in such a way that we may speak of it as an aggregate of persons clustered around an agnatic nucleus. The aggregation is linguistically identified with the nucleus by the designation of the village community to the lineage. It is only in reference to rules of exogamy and certain ritual activities that one needs to regard lineages as completely independent groups. This description shows that social life generally functions within local communities, regardless of size; from the village to the larger section.

Audrey (1969), gives a comparative example among the Bemba tribe in Zambia to explain kinship as a relationship based on a descent from the patrilineal and matrilineal lines unlike that of the Nuer. This is also true among many African tribes like the Bisa, Lamba, Lala, Chewa, Kaonde, and Luba, also from Zambia. Among these communities, a man's legal entitlements and rights of inheritance lie on his mother's side and none whatsoever. For example, a Bemba belongs to his mother's clan (umukoa), a group of relatives more or less distantly connected, who reckon descent from real or fictitious common ancestries, using a common totem name, and a series of praise titles, recite a common legend of origin and accept certain joint obligations (Audrey, 1969). This is not the case in the Nuer society where inheritance comes from paternal side. These scenarios point to the diverse norms and traditions of the African people.

The Nuer culture gives power to the lineage as the effective kinship unit. Marriage and the organization of family life revolves around this unit. An individual's legal entitlements and rights of inheritance are paternal. He has no rights on his maternal clan, except the right to acquire a portion of the bride wealth when his niece (*nyanyiman*) gets married. This practice is reciprocated by payment of the same amount of cattle when one of the nephews gets married. A Nuer inheritance belongs to his father's clan (*pekguändɛ*), and follows patrilineal lines among some other African societies. The matrilineal and patrilineal household and descent influence two major social activities: Succession and inheritance. A Nuer man inherits his dead father, maternal and paternal uncle, or brother. The inhabitants follow the trends of patrilineal cycle. Village headmen roles, court offices, ritual titles, and chieftainships are passed on in this way. Besides, social support is usually sought from the matrilineal or patrilineal line or descent group. For instance, the male head has control over children produced through the inheritance line. When a girl is getting married, both patri-lineage and matri-lineage relations are consulted. In many matrilineal societies, the maternal uncle is the go-between who undertakes all arrangements and responsibilities for his nephew's marriage whereas in case of a divorce, the maternal grandparents assume the responsibility of caring for the divorced couple's children.

It is noted that the patrilineal descent in a lineage, is inherited from the paternal relations whereas one's mother's family is recognized as consanguineal (blood-related) kin, but children do not belong to her family among the Nuer society, whereas in other societies such as in the Zambian communities highlighted above, the matrilineage inherited from the mother descent membership (Ayaya, 1976).

Kinship value (*Luot Maarä*)
Kinship value can be defined as ' 'the extended parental love which bind siblings, and is connected by bonds of marriage of the elementary family connecting them with one another into a network of relationships often refenced to as kinship system and affinity". Kinship value is the value of relationship essentially traced through parental links and recognizes for social purposes. It is a universal that can be found in all societies, but the extent of the value is limited in certain societies which recognize cognatic kinship within clan. The Nuer kinship value is stressed more to the patrilineal or agnatic kinship. Here parental love is a stronger value in the

mother line. In the case of the Nuer, parental love is the extending value in the father's line. The affinity value of relationships results from a marriage which links a person with his or her spouses' kin, e.g., the relative of his wife's sister or to his mother's brother's wife. Affinity value is the value of a parent, and brotherly love is extended to those whom a person is linked with through his or her spouse's kin, the relationship of a man to his wife's sister or to his mother's brother's wife. "The value of parental and brotherly love is so strong that the Nuer will call all who arc related to the father's brothers, as fathers, and all who arc related to the mother's sisters as mothers. The same is true for sons of his father's brother's sons as for his brothers. As noted, by Ayayo (1976), that "there is no term that distinguishes them; all are mothers, fathers, brothers, grandfathers, grandmothers and to give them another term will reduce that parental value". Kinship is reckoned through blood and betrothal (engagement and marriages) and it controls social relationships between people in a given community: it governs marital customs and regulations, determines the behaviour of an individual toward another (Mbiti, 1969). Indeed, this sense of kinship binds together the entire life of the community and it is event extended to animals, plants and non- living objects through the "totemic" system.

Totemic system of the Nuer
The totem is the visible symbol kinship unity of belongingness, of togetherness and common affinity. Almost all the concepts are connected with human relationship can be understood and interpreted through the kinship system. The totemism of Nuer people involves a selection of certain natural objects to the exclusion of others. Nuer totems are certain peculiar assortments such like; lion, waterbuck, monitor lizard, crocodile, various snakes, tortoise, ostrich, cattle egret, durra-birds, various trees, papyrus, gourd, various fish, red ant, river and stream, cattle with certain markings, monor- chids hide, rafter, rope and may include totemistic objects, parts of beasts and some diseases (Pritchard, 1956). There are spirits related to certain objects such as water spirit as part of mediation and understanding of God. This believe and practice is found among the western Nuer community of *Dok* from *Duong* sub clan. *Duong* has water spirit refers to as *Moth*. The community believe that *moth* could mediate to God through water spirit and is consulted when such need arises. For example, they offer sacrifices at the riverside to ensure safe passage of people or their livestock when crossing the Nile even if savaged crocodile infested does not pose threat when *moth* is consulted said one community elder from western Nuer.

Nuer do not have marked real element in their selection. Some animals, birds, fishes, plants and artifacts are absent from the list of their totems. Such creatures have excited the mythopoeic imagination of the Nuer and which figure most prominently in their folk-tales do not figure rarely and insignificantly, among their totems. It is to be noted that animals, birds, reptiles, and trees are symbols for Nuer of the relation of spirit to lineages, though not all, Nuer totems are in a general way highly regarded by all Nuer, on account of religious associations of one kind or another which have nothing to do with totemism as such. Hence, all Nuer have friendly feelings towards all birds and do not harm them because they are symbols of spirit and love by God. The Nuer may also be influenced in this matter by their belief that human twins are birds so that all twins respect all birds. The reason for this abstention is that the bird can fly in the skies and accordingly in communication with the "Great Spirit". For example, the pied crow (*Jakok in rol*) a bird which frequents Nuer homesteads and favoured because it is the bird of the female spirit (*buk*), the mother of *dɛng* which is respected by most Nuer people.

Nuer kinship is a network stretching horizontally in every direction, to embrace everybody in any given local group. This means that each individual is a brother or sister, father or mother, grandfather or grandmother, cousin or brother-in-law, uncle and so on. That means, everybody is related to everybody else, and there are many kinship terms to express the precise relationship pertaining between two individuals. When two strangers meet in the village, one of the first duties is to sort out how they may be related to each other, and having discovered how the kinship system implies to them, they behave to each other according to the accepted behaviour set down by the society. For example, two young people meet in a dancing place, male and female and wanted to talk about love but they discover that they are related, then they will treat each other as brother and sister, or as an old and younger brother; if they are uncle and nephew may be expected to give much respect to the uncle where this type of relationship is required by the society. It is possible also that from that moment on, the individual concerned will refer to each other by the kinship term, for instance" brother" "sister", "nephew"," uncle"," mother", with or without using their proper names. Such being the case then, a person has literally hundreds of" father", hundreds of "mothers", hundreds of "uncle" hundreds of" wives", hundreds of sons and daughters and so on.

The Nuer kinship system also extends vertically to include the departed and those yet to be born. It is part of traditional education for children in many Nuer societies to learn the genealogies of their descent. The genealogies give a sense of death, historically belongingness, a feeling of deep rootedness and a sense of sacred obligation to extend the genealogical line. Through genealogies, individual in the Nuer migration period from *Kuer - Kuong (Koat Liceh)* to the east of the Nile have firmly linked to those who have remained in the west of the Nile. Nuer considers genealogies as sacred means of orientation towards their communities where the foundation of different people lies. In some Nuer societies trace their genealogies as far back as the mythological first man such as "*Kang edowdow*", (mythological first man which some Nuer people in the east trace their genealogies back to), giving them a sense of pride and satisfaction.

The clan is the major sub-division of Nuer society. Some peoples may have up to a hundred families or more. Clan systems are by no means uniform in Nuer society. Evidence has shown that in African societies, there are patriarchal families where the descent is traced through the father such as the Nuer people of South Sudan; but there are also matriarchal family, in which descent is traced through the mother. Family are normally totemic, that is, each as an animal or part of it, a plant, a stone or mineral, which is regarded as it's totem and members of a particular family observes special care in treating or handling their totem, so that for example, they would not kill or eat it. The totem is the visible symbol of unity, kinship unity, of kinship, of belongingness, of togetherness and common affinity. Genealogies may be cited as far back as the original founder of the clan, if it has not been forgotten or if the genealogical line has not been broken through loss of memory.

Sharing the same view, Turaki (2006), argues that indeed kinship derives from the community, the belief that protection, meaning, identity and status derive from being an integral part of a community. In traditional Nuer thought, one cannot form a community with strangers or outsiders because one has no blood ties, nor ancestral affinity with them. The community has its origin and center in ancestry and kinship, and it is governed by kinship values: loyalty, affinity and obligations (Turaki, 2006). It is essentially moral and ethical and it is governed by the rules of behaviour and relationships. The defined kinship community, a territory, or class bound the sphere of influence of moral kinship among the Nuer. Those who are not part of the kinship community of the blood group are all part of the other community. Outsiders cannot expect to be treated in accordance with the same moral and ethical principles that prevail within the kinship community. In all matters the kinship community takes precedence over outsiders and strangers, who do not belong to them. This perception, gives the Nuer people an advantage and respect over their other Nilotic counter parts in terms of ethnicity extension which some scholars refer to as "Nuer expansion".

Rites of passage
Transition to adulthood has a special place and meaning among many communities worldwide because such progressions relate to the ceremonies at all milestones in life. Transition to maturity involves ceremonies of initiation, comparable to those at birth, which gives a person full responsibility within the society. People have different creative abilities at all stages and these have new effects. This premise is the reason different ceremonies through lifetime are structured differently. The concept of "growth" as a gradual coming into being or as an inclusive principle is an idea that is radically denied until an individual is properly incorporated in to the society through the rituals. These rites of passage to adulthoods have immediate significance for those involved. The change occurs as a result of the ceremonies. Bodily maturity is an external and nonessential phenomenon. In life, the essential aspect of growth is the spiritual, supernatural and mystical components. In many societies, there are ceremonies which make the boy an adult. Before these rites take place, the young man may not marry, participate in community deliberations or in war (Kristensen, 1968). Globally, these requirements for initiations are done to give the young man a spirit and new phase in life. Remarkably, transition is found almost in every culture religiously or culturally. The purpose of living in a society is to enhance human well-being of everyone while paying attention to the positive moral values that determine how the communities live and relate to each other.

A Nuer person's life begins at birth, through adolescence to full adulthood. They are formed to hold tenaciously to the belief in the ancestors, to revere them as powerful and benevolent members of the community in a mystical sense. Ancestors are held up as models to be aped in the effort to strictly adhere, preserve and transmit the traditions and norms of the community. The Nuer individual is psychologically equipped and motivated to promote the delicate balance and equilibrium believed to exist in the universe through ensuring harmony in his relationship with the invisible world and with members of the community. In a sense, the individual is a product of the community since a person is a unit of the larger corporate group. To Nuer, physical birth is not enough: the child must go through rites of incorporation so that it becomes fully integrated into the entire society. These rites continue throughout the physical life of the person, during which individual passes from one stage of corporates existence to another, for example, removing of lower teeth and initiation into adulthood.

Removing of lower teeth (*nak lɛc*)
The Nuer remove the four incisors as an initiation rite of passage for both boys and girls. The extraction of lower teeth of the children was such social event - initiation process leading into adulthood that takes different styles and ceremonies. They invariably remove the four lower canines as a sign of maturity. Hence, Nuer people of South Sudan do this traditionally as a sign of maturity.

Removing a young man's lower teeth are among the cultural practices marking the rites of passage in Nuer communities. Apart from that, Nuer believe that as the child matures with lower teeth his/her pronounciation ends with a hissing sound. To safeguard against that the Nuer thought is better to remove that source of hissing that tampers fluence in speaking. Previously, removing the lower teeth boys and young girls among the Nuer was done when they attained the ages of between 8 and 12 years. Historically, it was related that there was a sickness which used to attack children, long time ago before the Nuer moved to the Eastern side of River Nile. When the sickness attacks a child both lower and upper teeth bite the tongue and when unconscious may cut the tongue and sometimes leads to death. The disease was known as '*riɛny*' (meningitis). Certain accounts also suggest that the Nuer considered removing lower teeth to avoid identifying a person as cannibal (*lɛd* singular or *leed* plural). As such, teeth removal differentiated human beings from carnivores. A famous lore about cannibalism is the myth story of Gatluak Manguɛl, who the Nuer believe used to eat people. He was said to be originally from the Alliab/Atwot Dinka who originated from Western Nuer. Teeth removal likewise made it easy to identify children during wars. One Nuer elder narrated that removing the lower teeth was done to minimize injuries among fighting children. He added that these youngsters prefer to fight by biting each other, which may sometimes result in severe injuries. These practices are nowadays fading away due to growing human interaction with different cultures and modernization. Folklore shows that these rituals serve ornamental purposes and identify individual from different ethnic groups. While the practices are specific to certain ethnic groups, some have adopted them from other cultures. For instance, the central and eastern Nuer adopted face tattooing (*bier*) from the Annyuak and Murle ethnic communities.

Tattoos *(Bieer*)
The Nuer are very particular about body cleanliness; the hair is constructed into two structures that give the impression of figures of hair on the head. They wear beads, and other decoration which include cutting dots on forehead and tattooing on the body. This is said to have been adapted from the Anyuak and Murle ethnic communities as mentioned above. First, by the eastern Nuer and then spread over throughout the Nuerland, especially, doted pattern which are common among the Bul Nuer men and females. The Nuer have evolved a culture that honours the self and this is expressed in body and facial marks, speech, song, music, dance, poetry during the social events such as marriage and other ceremonies.

However, since traditional institutions and social behaviour are evolving, some of these practices have been abandoned and are no longer part of the Nuer standard practices. These changes are partly due to that the Nuer resorted to take their children to schools to acquire modern education in lieu of their traditional options. Besides, children who have gone to school these days are proud to have their lower teeth intact a privilege of enjoying life's pleasures such as enjoying a slab of steak. Increased public health awareness by government health institutions and aid organizations on health risks posed by teeth removal is also to blame for the dwindling prominence of the practice. The Nuer now know that teeth removal may lead to the spread of infectious diseases. Wars and migration are another reason. These factors have compelled the Nuer adopting other cultures as well.

Because of these recent developments, removing of lower teeth and tattooing among the Nuer are now considered negative practices. This premise has been reinforced by educational knowledge which the Nuer society cherishes as a transforming instrument in this changing world. This undesirable practice is almost disappearing in urban settings. However, it is still prominent in specific rural settings where families, traditional, and spiritual leaders force individuals to uphold the rituals. Moreover, these cultural practices, which were being perceived as positive in the past are now disappearing. I have noted that the Nuer, despite resisting the effort of colonial authorities to change the traditional practice of removing teeth, have only now responded by accepting to let their children's teeth be intact.

Initiation (*gäri*) into adulthood
Initiation (*Gäri*) refers to the stage of child's incorporation of his social existence to adulthood among the Nuer. The Nuer receive facial markings called (*gäär*) as part of their initiation into adulthood. This pattern of Nuer scarification varies, however, one among the 'gared' (scarified) group is given seven marks to give him the leadership of that group. In some situations he could be a maternal uncle's son within specific sub-groups. The most common initiation pattern among males consists of six parallel horizontal lines which are cut across the forehead with a knife (*ngom*), often with a dip in the lines above the nose. The process involves get-together of family members, relatives, and friends. This stage, revealed that all male Nuer young men are initiated from boyhood to manhood through a special ritual known as *gäri*. Boys are usually initiated in to adulthood when they attain the ages of between 14 and 16 years. In the olden days, this rite of passage happened when the boys were somewhat older, say, between 16 and 18 years. The initiation ceremony is considerably more complex among the Nuer and the age-set system has a greater social importance compared to other South Sudanese Nilotes. At the initiation stage, the young male person is fully integrated into adulthood, gaining rights and obligations in family. At the same time, the entire society gets to recognize the young adult's age set (see Figure no: 6 below).

Figure 3: showing age mate scarified (initiated) young men

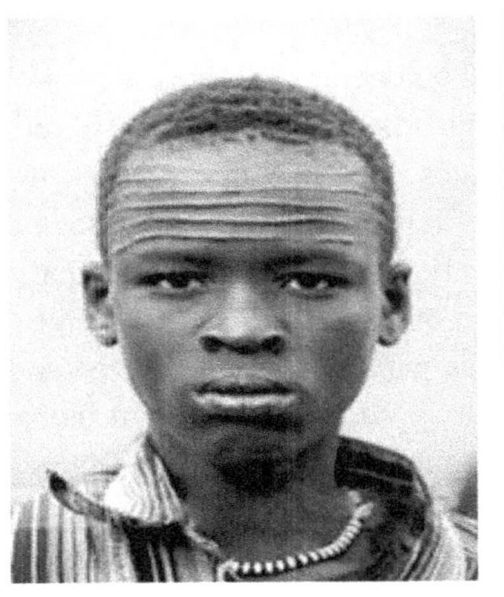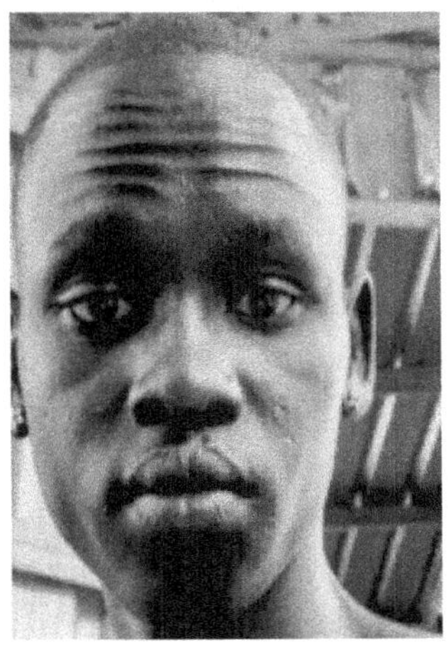

Photo by: Author

Family (*Gɔl*)

Mbiti (1969), states that in the African traditional society the family has a much wider circle of members compared to the European or North American societies (Mbiti, 1969). The Nuer family includes grandparents, parents, children, uncles and aunties and their immediate relatives. In many areas, extended families are a real phenomenon and this set up establishes families in one compound or close to one another. The joint households are one large family. The number of family members may range from ten to hundreds of people and it is possible several wives may belong to one husband. It is the practice in some societies to send children to live for some months or years with relatives, and those children are counted as members of the families where they happen to live.

In the Nuer society, the family includes the departed relatives, who are designated as the living dead, *plural jɔɔk/singular jɔah.* Their names suggest that they are, alive in the memories and share with their surviving families. Besides, the Nuer believe that their dead kinship remains interested in the affairs of the family they left behind. The Nuer have a culture of tracing back their ancestral lineage to reflect their family tree to several generations where one belongs. For example, the genealogy of certain section of the Nuer was assumed to be originating from the tree and such community must respect that particular tree as sacred and believe in it. Surviving members of the family must not forget the departed ones for fear that misfortune may befall them or their relatives. The older a person lived on earth, the longer he is remembered and regarded as an integral part of a human family. People give offerings of food and libation to the living dead because they are still a part of the family. These offerings are a token of the fellowship, communion, remembrance, respect and hospitality, extended to those who are immediate pillars of the family. The living dead solidify and mystically bind the whole family. The Nuer people believe that the departed members of the family visit by appearing in dreams. During such incidents, the living dead inquire about family affairs. They may also warn against danger, rebuke the living for their indiscretion or ask for food, usually meat and a drink. The Nuer believe that an offended living dead can revenge or demand a rectification.

Aside from the intriguing beliefs about the living dead, the Nuer concept of the family includes; the unborn members still in the loins of the living. They are the buds of hope and expectation, each family makes sure that its existence is not extinguished. The family provides for its continuation, and prepares for the coming of those not yet born. This premise is the reason why Nuer parents are anxious to see their children find husbands and wives. A parent whose children failed in finding mates are considered killers of the family lineage.

The household is the smallest unit of the family and consists of the parents and their children. In certain instances, it includes grandparents. One might refer to such a unit as *family at night*, for it is generally at night that the household sit around a fire at home. At night they spend time with their children in the house discussing family affairs and relate stories. The parents educate their children about domestic relationships and culture. The narrative above highlights the place of the Nuer family as the primary social group with the core role of forming responsible leadership for the entire community. Therefore, individuals Nuer begin life in the family and return to it in old age. Nuer individual takes responsibility to cultivate responsible leadership. Besides, she/he is discouraged from blaming others for his/her shortcomings.

The household in Nuer is the western societies' equivalent of a family. This statement implies that a man who has two or more wives, has many households because each wife usually has her house. The compound occupied by one household is a village, which includes houses, gardens or fields, granaries and the courtyards. In rare cases, villages also have threshing ground, the men's outdoors fire place (in some societies), and the children's playground and family shrines. Some societies have the village surrounded by a fence, which essentially makes it a single household or family. Most Nuer traditional houses are built around in pyramid shape which forms a village of several houses for living and kraal (*Luak*) where cattle are kept during the rainy seasons. The houses generally face the center of the compound with a general orientation towards the main entrance to the village.

The Nuer society is exogamous. Family members do not intermarry. However, some migrants who have joined that family and become part of the clan are allowed to marry within the clan. The size of a clan varies considerably. Some clans are made up of several thousand people while others have only a hundred or so members. An individual is born to a clan; a permanent identity she cannot change. However, marriage may change or weaken the clan's membership. In some societies, every family has separate land areas. Other societies prefer to have the families intermingle. Because of the living arrangements of some villages, it is possible to tell an individual by the name of his or her locality. For instance, *Gaatkiir* is a common name among the western and eastern Jikäny Nuer. Apart from localizing the sense of kinship, clan systems provide closer human co-operation, especially in times of need.

When internal conflicts erupt, clan members join one another to fight their aggressive neighbor. An individual whose land in trouble finds easy help from relatives, especially in situations such as paying fines levied on accidental incidents. Accidental wounded or killing are examples of such incidents whose fines elicit help from relatives. Today, trends of collective responsibilities are likened to giving financial support to students studying in institutes of higher education. Some Nuer societies have gone ahead to divide their clans into sub-clans or *gates*, usually, as a level between the family and the clan. These localized clans deal with affairs which need not take up the collective time of the whole clan. These subdivisions, over the course of time, grow into full-fledged clans. The *gate* comprises of members from a common ancestor dating up to eight or ten generations back. The Nuer have structures that respect ancestral lineage and they strictly observe genealogical tracing of generations. For example, one may be a member of a small lineage that traces its descent only to his grandfather and live next to another lineage whose grandfather was different. But both lineages are related at the level of a fourth or higher-generation ancestor, which allows them to consider themselves kin and under the right circumstances they might collaborate.

The concept of "_Ruic/Ruiy_" (leadership) among the Nuer
Generally, leadership can be described as the ability of an individual to influence, motivate and enable others to contribute towards the effectiveness and success of community of which a person belongs. This sub-section presents the concept of leadership among the Nuer people of South Sudan. It begins with the qualification of being a leader concerned about the necessity of reconciliation by use of Nuer traditional justice systems that involve truth and justice that leads to harmony among his community. They are the communities' key decision makers whose requirements are taken seriously by their societies each having qualifications which to some extent expected to be a person with religious knowledge and power of oratory.

Qualification of a Nuer leader
In order to be a leader among the Nuer, one must be respected in the community. He is expected to be full of wisdom and understanding in decision making. To some extent, he should have traditional backing of power and authority. Power and authority refer to mysterious powers that may foresee and lead to wise judgment in resolving issues. He must have family a wife/wives because true leadership among the Nuer starts from home. Leaders are sometime members and representatives of a particular clan within the community although, assimilated individuals from other communities with similar leadership qualities are permitted to lead. They should be persons who must be acquainted with the Nuer cultural and traditional justice system beginning with the family, clan and the community as whole. Such leaders, are expected to be lovers of peace, and loyal to taboos of the community. Nuer community hold that traditional justice system is established on the sovereignty of their socio-cultural settings. Among the Nuer, a leaders must possess certain characteristics and qualities: generosity, integrity, self-awareness, ability to communicate, influential, empathetic, decisive, brave to stand and speak on behalf of his people and keep unity at all times also he is expected to be generous by giving people food if available.

Nuer Unity (_Mat Nuärä_)
The first question any Nuer person would ask, is why were the Nuer united and to make their way through by assimilating other communities and resisted the colonial invaders to the point that they become famous in the world history? Where the Nuer lawlessness, make them unable to govern themselves? No! The Nuer had their own system of managing themselves (self government) without fear or favour in the past. We have noted earlier that the Nuer lived in small communities and managed their own affairs for the good of their society, unlike negative developments seen in Nuer Nation today. There were four reasons that make the Nuer to keep unity. First, cultural identity: The themes of Nuer unity, cultural identity and resistance to foreign invasion thus, became crucial in such a symbolic unity for their survival. The dynamics of this value suggests a protective moral for the preservation of the community and the values that define it. The Nuer value this kind of unity as we see in many of their sectional's activities that governs their migration to the east of the Nile at the time, focused on this important traditional value despite external threats. Second, threats posed by external forces: Sometimes this value of unity is threatened by external forces. For example, the invasion of foreign forces kept them together in a circle is symbolic of the unity that exists among them while inside the circle symbolizes the evil forces working against the unity of the Nuer people around this

circle. This is a demonstration of the importance of being united as a people which the Nuer perceived as their strengths and power. It involves sharing ideas together and symbolizes joint struggle against a foe, pursuing an opponent together when confronted. This has been a historical fact among the Nuer who used to live in small communities, but, unite against any external forces when aggressed. Third, value of communality: Nuer values are in line with their concepts of communality and kinship systems. This unity is manifested in times of crisis in the community particularly during scarcity, funerals and when members of the community need support. It should be recalled that the Nuer people lived in a clan system as discussed earlier in this text and this made it easy for individual member of the community to identify with his fellow kinsmen. This unity becomes significant to the holistic development of the Nuer, communicating cultural values, to physical and moral development. As their children grow up these days, they play, sing and dance and learn various topics about their culture. They are taught a common ancestry which creates their belonging. Hence, at a tender age they are socialized to respect these relatives. The Nuer have much respect for their family ties, which give them a sense of unity and belonging. Children show this unity and belonging as they sing about their kinship system when they gathered. They recognize that the destiny of their community is crucial. This communality educates children on the value of a common family tree, which calls for dignity and togetherness which becomes crucial value in ensuring that every member of the community is taken care of. This way children grow up in a community set-up and are expected to know how they relate to other members of the society.

Finally, a fundamental aspect of identity is the Language (*Thok Naath)*: Nuer language is another unifying factor within their communication networks. *Thok Naath* is what the Nuer use and are proud of, all over their Nation, from west of the Nile, central and eastern Nuer with no difficulty in communicating. It has been noted from previous researchers such as famous pioneer Evans-Pritchard on Nuer and Howell, both had shown no disparities on the Nuer language when compiling their research works. A meeting with the elders throughout Nuer region text revealed that the language is homogenously spoken. This shows the unity of Nuer/Naath people using one language (*Thok Naath)* as a uniting factor; unlike other Nilotic groups such as the Dinka who have different Bible translations due to variation of dialects. Thus, *Thok Naath* is one of the common influences that unites the Nuer society as a whole and this unity links them with concept of leadership (*ruic*) among the Nuer.

As we note from Lewis's analysis, pointing out the importance of the institution "*Ruic*" among the Nuer that it had not received consideration it deserved from the anthropologies. During his interaction with Lɔu Nuer leaders, he was overwhelmed with the importance which they attached to the institution of "*Ruiic*" noting that Lɔu Nuer spoke of four successive "*Ruic*"*(rueec Lɔkä)* leaders of the Lɔu Nuer: Bidit Biliu Yol, nicknamed as Bidiit Kweinyang who led the Lɔu to their present territory; Bec Chol (Bec Cotlieth), a very famous cattle chief who latter inherited leadership from Bidit Biliu Yol after his passing on and led Lɔu Nuer to Bongjaak, Yout Nyakoaŋ (Dinka by origin), a noted Leopard Skin Chief. Yout Nyakong was the youngest brother of Pakuol Nyakong, but Pakuol was denied leadership by Nyal Beliu who at the time had spiritual authority to make decisions during their migration period. This angered Pakuol and decided to go further north and joined Turkey forces with whom he came back some years latter to Pulturuk (Lɔu area) and uncessfully attempted to take over the leadership of his brother. This time the conflict was in Pulturuk the leadership of his brother Yuot Nyakoang with the help of the foreign government (*Turuk*). The leadership contest between the two brothers (Yuot and Pakuol) took place ealier in Atar where they stayed for three years before moving further east according to traditional source and finally, we noted the leadership of Ngundɛng Bong of the Pyramid who was a great Prophet as well as a Leopard Skin Chief.

Jal (2013) noted some of these leaders too, and added that the Lɔu Nuer were under the leadership of a *Kuär Thɔach* (River or Water Chief), Bidiit Char, popularly known as Bidiit Kueinyaŋ, led the Lɔu migration to the Zaraf island, crossing the Bahr el-Jebel to the east at *Waath Yokä* (ford) and subsequently settling in the northern half of the island in what is now called Juach Boor, where they pushed out the Ngok Dinka and split them into two main groups as well as driving them out from their own area of interaction. Those Dinka were two sections: one was led by Lual Ayak, crossed the Bahr el Zaraf to the east and the other group was led by Kuol Arou, who crossed to the west and settled in Abyei on the Behr el Arab in the South-western Kordofan region (Jal, 2013). This narrative was also confirmed by some Nuer elders I had conversation with in a group discussion, who told me that the above leaders were very important functionaries, empathizing that the role of great Prophet Ngundɛng Bong whose legacy is being felt, was, and still very important within the Nuer leadership structure. Noted also, is the concept of *"Ruic"- Rueec* (Authority) as relates to Prophets, remained as a central institution in the Nuer political system at the time and even today.

The latter's songs of Prophet Ngundɛŋ, continued being told in form of songs and prophecies as unifying influences among the Nuer and also their neighbors and being seen as relevance in the current political system in South Sudan. The colonial wars (resistance) and current conflicts including the separation of South Sudan are found in these prophecies and songs. I happened to be a research assistant in mid 1970s for Douglas Johnson who has written extensively about the Nuer Prophets and other texts on Sudan and South Sudan. I was his interpreter and latter transcribed most of those songs and prophecies. Though, I do not claim any authority, I have learned and treasured some of these historical documentations, like some of my Nuer colleagues who did the same work with Douglas; like Ustaz Kun Puoc. Lewis also confirmed some of these sectional leaders, mentioning that the first government expedition to Lɔu Nuer in 1905 wrote of Ngundɛŋ as Chief of the Lɔu Nuer, reported that he had succeeded Yuot Nyakoang. Similar early investigations in Lɔu Nuer, Military Inteligence Reports (M.I.R.) in the Zeraf (Fangak) had given similar outcomes. As noted earlier that Pritchard gave very little prominence to the *"Ruiic"* in his thesis on the Nuer, although he stressed the political importance of the Prophets amongst the Nuer resistance to the government. He noted the position of Latjjɔɔr and Bidiit who led Jikäny and Lɔu on their great colonizing invasions, now considered them as leaders who stood and spoke for their people than was previously thought.

Bough Käpɛl (Gaawäär Leader) was one of the Nuer great leaders who prearranged and dispatched an expedition across the Bahr el Jebel to the east, apparently to survey the region. When the report of expedition had been received, Buogh ordered Gaawäär to migrate to the Zaraf Island in about 1820. The Gaawäär chose their leader Bough Käpel to lead them across the River Nile to acquire new land from the Dinka. In a ritual cermoney, the people lifted him on high so that God might see that he had been chosen and they gave him a gourdful of milk to drink into which they had all spat (Pritchard, 1956). This was a sign of pleading to God to bless him, although blessing can also be given without spitting. Religious significance of blessing lies in a dominant motive of Nuer religion as blessings are thought to be effective only because God make them happen. In Gaawäär the Käpel family of Leopard Skin Chiefs had for many decades supplied the "*Ruiic*" (leadership) until their numbers grew larger and the latter split into two communities of *Radh* and *Barr*, from whom *Deng* Lekä and family then became leaders of Barr- Gawäär sub-section.

The emergence of Latjɔɔr Duach, popularly known as Latjɔɔr Diŋyian as a leader of Jikäny Nuer later came with some difficulties when a woman called Man-Leng inherited leadership from her husband called Dol Thiang. This emerged at a time when there was a great demand for additional territory as well as the need for a strong leadership. Latjɔɔr Duach (*Latjɔɔr Diŋyian*) became a legendary culture hero during the Jikany migration working on the background. He appealed to Man-Leng Dol who was a diviner and leader of Jikany Nuer to step down but she did not give up her position despite the leadership challenges that were being foreseen by Latjɔɔr Dingyian. However, with the mysterious passing on of Man-leng, the way was clear for Latjɔɔr to succeed her and this, as noted by Jal (2013), Latjɔɔr leadership was soon blessed at a meeting of the council of Nuer elders (*duol diitni*), which was convened mainly for that purpose. According to one Nuer Elder David Ruon Majiok, after securing blessings from the council of elders, Latjɔɔr began preparations for the Jikany migration to the east. First, he invited a ritual experts; *Kuär muon,* and *guän tang* (war master) to bless his journey demonstrate the significance of leadership in accordance to the Nuer customs. Second, he made a search for a diviner to help carry out his mission. He then found Nyaguëc (diviner) who was also named *Boorietcäng* (*Boor Malual*); and after performing successful rituals needed, he decided to marry her, not because of creation, but to help him during his expedition to the east as a diviner. She eventually made him successfully cross the River Nile at *Wath ŋöök* in Fashoda in Chollo Kingdom. Third, Latjɔɔr established an understanding in the east with an important person called Padiet Gakgak to secure support of his early mission. These were important steps before Latjɔɔr started his expedition to eastern Nuer (*Jikäny*).

Before setting out his journey to the east, Latjɔɔr invited a number of ritual experts: the *wut yɔɔk, Kuär muɔɔn, guän thoach and guän tang* (war master) mainly to bless his journey (Jal, 2013). This shows the importance of leadership (*ruic*) in the Nuer customs In the Nuer customs each clan manages its own internal affairs through the arbitration of a *duol diitni* (council of elders) while maintaining unity with other clans for their collective defense against their neighbors. This is an indication that collective solidarity is by no means confined to small clan segments in so far as ecological conditions forced them to live together where the feeling of "unity of purpose and that of necessity" prevails. The sense of common identity and the creation of a priest by "hand" -investing of priestly power on a *duek* (lay person) by a community was a common feature. For example, among the Gaawäär Nuer, during their migration, settlement and expansion mentioned earlier to their eastern land, Buogh Kapel was elected as *primus inter pares* by a council of elders and was made as *Kuär muon* (land priest) at a ceremony in which he was lifted up to *Kuoth* (god) by his community on the ground that Käpel clan has blood relationship with Gɛɛ who was the original *Kuär Muɔɔn* of the Nuer/*Naath* community that conducted a ritual ceremony at *Koat Liech* before Gëë and the *Hääk* separated (Jal, 2013).

Around 1828, migrants from the ancestral Jikäny confederation launched the most fortunate of these sojourns, distilled their collective understanding of their ancestors' migration to eastern *Jikäny* (their present land), after consolidating the spiritual, logistical, and political resources necessary to mobilize a migration to eastern Nile (*kiir känycäŋ*) before Jikäny Nuer left their homeland of Cieŋ Taŋ west of the Nile, relatively open area beyond Collo territory, organizing alliances and spiritual political arrangements that Latjɔɔr leveraged to mobilize migrants for that venture. Latjɔɔr first established an understanding in the east vital to the success of this early mission with an important host called Padiet Gakgak from Doŋjol Dinka and also secured the supernatural support of a powerful Jikäny spiritual figure (Nyaguëc) to bless and protect the new Jikäny community leadership. Latjɔɔr alliances with Padiet and Nyaguëc established a precedent for collaboration with resident communities that migrants continued to emulate throughout the following decades.

Padiet Gakgak came from a prominent local family and had a reputation as a formidable warrior who carried a unique and supernaturally lethal weapon (a conventional Nilotic Spear with an axe head attached, somewhat reminiscent of giant (huge). Nuer traditions suggest that Padiet Gakgak was impressed with Latjɔɔr's bravery and had less reason to worry about the unpropriatiated Doŋjol ghosts haunting Padiet Gakgak. Some Nuer leaders suggest that Padiet Gakgak was also more interested in recruiting allies to replace some of the many Padaŋ lost in the early 1820s to the flood and to collo raiders. The two men then made a pact that gave Latjɔɔr access to the empty floodplains east of the elevated banks the Sobat River and west of the seasonal *Yal* or *Khor Adar* (Stringham, 2016).

Secondly, there was concern from Latjɔɔr's fellow Jikäny about their inability to cross to alien land (east of the Nile) as other Nuer confederations had already done (Gaawäär and Lɔu Nuer). Because of this leadership gap, Latjɔɔr had to speed up looking for someone who had a reputation as a seer (that is, *tiët* or "diviner" known for their ability to see and converse with spirits inside gourds) to bless his mission. Latjɔɔr held a contest to see if any "seer" could find an axe head that he pretended he had lost. According to Nuer oral traditions, numerous diviners failed to find the missing axe, until a post-menopausal matriarch named Nyaguëc (Boorietcang or *Boor Malual*); proved her worth by "seeing" that the axe was not lost but hidden within his thick, matted hair while others said it was under armpit

After Nyaguëc demonstrated her clairvoyance Latjɔɔr began looking for a way to secure her spiritual powers for the venture to the east and eventually found a way to do so by altering Nuer ideas about marriage to become as one family acquiring the right to benefit from the procreative powers of another family's daughter. In this case, Latjɔɔr was not interested in having children by Nyaguëc, as she was already old for child-bearing. But Latjɔɔr respected her supernatural insights and wanted to benefit from her spiritual wisdom. After the wedding,

Nyaguëc's prophecies that Latjɔɔr's party would acquire large herds convinced many Jikäny, and a number of Bul to the west, to join his troop. The couple recruited important officiants they needed to organize a Nuer colony, including Jaaŋ Win (a *wut yɔɔk* or "man of cattle: who had the authority to preform *gaar*) and a Bul war-song leader (*kit*) named Wɛcyiel Gual. Traditional sources suggest that Nyaguëc and Latjɔɔr secured the support of the most powerful of all Jikäny divinities, WIU, by persuading the current guardian of this Sacred Spear, Diet Nyak, to bless their venture. The couple also scored a strategic victory when they convinced some of their northern neighbors in the *Kwil* (*Kuel*) section of the Ruweŋ confederation of *Jiëëŋ* on the Sudd's northern edge to join their expedition. Nyaguëc avoided confrontations with both Nuer (Lak and Thiaŋ confederations) and *jiëëŋ* (Rut, Thoi, and Luäc) whose territories lay across the more direct route eastward.

Jikäny Nuer migrants reached a place opposite a *jiëëŋ* settlement called *Jal-yɔɔk* then in the territory of the Nyiɛl section of the Doŋjol Dinka community of the Padaŋ), they spotted a blue heron (*ŋöök*) standing on a mid-stream sandbar, and launched this revealed shallow part of the river "Blue Heron Port" (*Wath ŋöök*). It was this time that Nyaguëc helped Jikäny through this ordeal by securing divine favor. However, the community paid an awful price. At Blue Heron Port, Nyaguëc said to kill a person for the journey and take out the bile and smear it on the grass. The person slain was called Tiam Dhɔr Joc, a man of Cieŋ Rɛŋ (from Gaa-jak Jikäny). People sat beside the river because they feared the river. A blue heron came and walked in the river. People entered the river and it was called *Wath ŋöök.* Tiam Dhɔr Joc, the sacrificial victim, became the most famous casualty of a campaign that had avoided human resistance so successfully that its greatest test proved to be a natural one (Stringham, 2016). Latjɔɔr Dingyian's leadership with a lot of internal problems finally crossed the River Nile and settled first in Guel Guk area being the Jikany home land in the east.

This institution (*Ruiic*), in so far as it existed, was elective and not hereditary they were the charismatic leaders who came to the fore in times of crisis and naturally these crises were mainly the result of war. Any (Nuer) community were politically active when making war for its own survival and it was mainly in this connection that the term "*Ruiic*" seems to have been that of an orator; the mouthpiece in fact for that particular community, finding words to express the feelings of the group and oratorical powers, therefore, seem to have been the chief qualification for the position at the time. With these explanations, Lewis later contended that if these people were at one and the same time "*Rueec*" (leaders) and Leopard Skin Chief, the disagreement between Corriat and Pritchard on the importance of the Leopard Skin Chief noted earlier was now clarified and therefore, ruic (authority) remains as important institution among the Nuer political development.

CHAPTER FOUR:
MARRIAGE AMONG THE NUER

Courtship

The Nuer people are exogamous society and traditionally, marriage was an elaborate matter. It began with courtship between the girl and the man and once an agreement to marry was reached the matter was reported to the parents and if acceptable on grounds of class, social, and other criteria, the groom party have to pay dowry through negotiation processes known as (*Twɔc yɔɔk*). Such marriage practices are among the community's most important cultural covenants. According to Nuer traditions, a newly married woman would leave her father's household and take up residence with her new husband. However, she does not make the move immediately. Instead, the customs dictates that she stays with her parents for about a year or so, and sometimes until she conceived. This arrangement proceeded even though the marriage process had been completed. The reason for keeping a betrothed woman at her paternal household for such a period served to allow her family enough time to induct her into the life of matrimony. As one Nuer Elder Puok Ruathdɛl explains: during the time in question, the bride would receive instructions from her mother and other elderly women on how to behave when she gets to her new home.

Meanwhile, the husband would do the same under the guidance of his parents. The conclusion of the marriage process ended when dowry or some part of dowry of the agreed cattle is paid. Usually, the numbers of cattle vary from clan to the other but ranges from between 20 to 40 on average. A girl with certain physical attributes and large family received more dowry than others. The Nuer believed in physical features to mar beauty. For example, a tall and brown girl with gap in the teeth which the Nuer believed that such physical attributes are a sign of beauty and good character. After this stage, a wedding ceremony was conducted, concluding the process, which unites the bride and the groom to their new home but, observing the customs.

According to Nuer customs bridge wealth is perceived in its structural perspective which is in terms of lineages. Children are attached by payment of bride wealth to the lineage of their father and are known as children of the cattle of the man in whose name they were paid, and they become joints in his branch of descent. The man in whose name the cattle were paid is always their pater, the lineage father. If he dies, the widow should be inherited by close relative that is to say, by one of the brothers to her husband. But even should a widow decline to cohabit with one of her husband's paternal kin and prefer to live as a concubine with some man unrelated to her dead husband, any children she may bear are the late's children. Every child must have a pater or, which is saying the same thing among the Nuer, belong to a lineage, and if an unmarried woman has a child it is legitimatized either by subsequent payment of bride wealth or by payment of a fine (Pritchard, 1956). There are two important functions of bride wealth in Nuer society which include the role in creating new social ties between persons and regulating the interrelations between these persons till such time as their relationships become assimilated to kinship patterns largely and the role in the kinship system and its structural part in interline age relations.

Polygamy
The limitation to this section of the text is the term polygamy. The term polygamy is both formal and informal in the Nuer customs. This shows how broad the term is and will only cover types of polygamy applicable to the Nuer in this text. Whenever the term polygamy is used, it simply means a man with more than one wife. But there are other types of polygamy marriage such as; ghost marriage, the levirate marriage, marriage of a barren woman and widow's inheritance.

Polygamy is an umbrella term that refers to the state of having more than one spouse at the same time. Polygamy is the practice of a male having multiple female spouses, which for sometimes had been the only form practiced on a significant basis and will inform the main subject of discussion in this text with some of its types. Pritchard (1951), defines polygamous family as a unit where the husband marries several wives but the children of each wife belong exclusively to her hut and to her cooking fire, so that the polygamous family is divided into a number of separate domestic groups within the larger whole. The huts of these wives are the center of these elementary families which have a common husband and father. Outside her hut each woman has a mud windscreen, against which she makes her cooking fire and near to it is her a plastered hole, (*thoŋ)* in the ground for pounding grain. This mud screen, the top of which is fashioned into three humps, is sign of a married woman's status as the mistress of her home and the mother of children, just as the hearth in the byre is the sign of a man's status as the father of a family and the master of a household and herd (Pritchard, 1951).

Polygamy marriages are common among the Nuer if the man can afford to provide for multiple wives. Marrying more than one wife sometimes indicate wealth. During early days, most society in South Sudan major wealth was in term of having many wives; many children, and many cattle. In some areas, children are looked at as an auxiliary factor, and most people tend to cling to the notion of many wives and many children for the greater production, and an increase in wealth and prestige. In most instances, women have rank or standard of respect in the family level according to the seniority, and respect gained from husband. (Garvey, 2015). Among the Nuer, the desire for children is usually very high, and most often women who had more girls never give up producing children for the fact that they may have chance to get a baby boy. This practice was/is deep-rooted in the traditional Nuer society, as children were seen to be a form of pride and wealth, thus a family with more offspring was considered well endowed. As such, polygamy was used to build strong empires and a continuation of such. The Nuer also embraced polygamy through widow inheritance meant to care for orphans. In some instances, the Nuer traditional women allowed their husbands to marry co-wives to help with division of labour as they were expected to till farmlands. They also consented to such unions to ease the burden of child-bearing, thus they felt more secure in polygamous unions.

Ghost Marriage (*Kuen Ciek Jɔkä*)
Ghost marriage, among the Nuer people is perceived as the means of providing a wife an offspring for a man who has died without ever having married. The kin of an unmarried man who dies have a duty to look for a man among them who will marry for his brother a wife and in this way, the memory of the deceased brother will be kept alive and he can make his wants

known in the dreams of the children born to him by means of this ghost marriage. Neglect by his kin of this duty is believed to result in the deceased haunting them. The main difference between ghost marriage and levirate, which is also practiced by the Nuer, is this: in levirate, the woman was married to the deceased during his lifetime and this marriage continues after his death, whereas in a ghost marriage, she was not married to him during his lifetime, but only after his death.

Nuer custom dictates that an unmarried male relative of the deceased stand in as husband until a male heir is born. Formal marriage ceremony is contracted, and the dead man is regarded as the head of the family and any child obtained from this kind of marriage is recognized as being the child of the deceased man. Once a male heir is born, the ghost marriage ends and the man is freed to start his own family but remain obligated to provide for the deceased's family. The dead man's wealth whether inherited or provided by the family remains within his own family and his widow is protected from economic hardship. The Nuer also believe that unless a man produces a male heir, his ghost will haunt his family bringing misfortune if no son was produced in his name. Thus, a wealthy family may marry for a deceased son to retain his name and lineage, instead of giving it up after death.

The levirate marriage among the Nuer
The levirate is a specific law for a specific situation. In Scripture, it is found that the patriarchs practiced it, Moses commanded it and the Jews may well have practiced it in the time of Jesus because the Jews referred to it when testing Jesus in Matthew 22:23. The levirate marriage, comes into play when a family experiences the loss of a member. As such, the levirate offers an opportunity to study the family at a moment of breakdown and restructuring and also offer an attempt to mend that which had been broken, reconstituting one part of a family by rearranging its members and realigning their relationship to each other. Unlike Islam's unique construct of the levirate results in the creation of an entirely new family rather than reforming the one broken by the husband's death because an individual man or woman's primary obligations should be to an existing spouse rather than to the extended family, as represented by a deceased spouse or sibling.

The purpose of the levirate marriage among the Nuer is to ensure that the lineage of a man who dies without being able to produce an heir would not die out. This concern for ensuring the continuation of the lineage of the deceased is understandable for in Israel it was regarded as a great misfortune for a man to die without male issue. This accounts for people turning to polygamy, adoption and other methods in the bid to have a male child (Davies, 1981). This preservation of a man's 'name', according to Burrows (1940), involved at least three things: It involved the provision of an heir for his property so that it might be kept in the family and in the normal line of inheritance. It involved also the continuation of his personal life in the life of his son according to a deep-seated conception of the ancient world (Burrows 1940). To this may be added the idea of welfare in the hereafter as dependent upon the performance of ancestral rites by the descendants. For a man who left no son, there would be nobody on earth to perform these rites. The firstborn son of a levirate marriage would be reckoned as the heir of the deceased brother.

Marriage of a barren woman (*kuen ciek mi ruol*)

The union in which a woman marries another woman is rare amongst the Nuer society, though, it is publicly practiced and they are regarded as simple marriages with the male partner being involved (Pritchard, 1951). When the marriage rites have been completed the husband gets a male kinsman to beget children by her wife and to assist, regularly or when assistance is particularly required, in those tasks of the home of carrying out of which a man is required. The father is referred to as the pater. A third person, the genitor, is required to impregnate the wife. He could be a friend, neighbour or kinsman of the pater and would help around in the home for tasks, which are deemed, unfit for women to do. For the marriage to become official, the pater has to pay a bride wealth to the wife, as would happen if a man were to marry a woman. The woman who marries in this way is normally barren, and for this reason counts in some respects as a man. She acquires cattle through the marriage of kinswomen, including some of those due to uncles on the marriage of a niece, or by inheritance, she counts as a man in these matters. She is the legal husband and can demand damage if they have relations with other men without her consent. She is the pater of their children and on the marriage of their daughters she receives the cattle of the father and her brothers and sisters receive the other cattle which go to the father's side in the distribution of bride wealth as the custom allows. Her children are called after her as though she were a man. She administers her home and herds as a man would, being treated by her wives and children with the deference they would show to a male husband and father. This is done among the Nuer for creation purposes, unlike western style of Lesbians partnership.

Foster marriages amongst the Nuer

In Nuer parlance, inheritance has different meanings. It is considered as property left behind for the heirs, wife and agnatic relatives of the family. Inheritance should not be seen only as the entrance of living persons into the possessions of dead relatives, nor should it be seen as a succession to all rights of the deceased. Rather, it is to be considered as the transference of the status from the dead to the living with respect to specific property objects. According to Nuer traditions, wife inheritance, as a man marrying a wife to the name of the dead kinsman and it is not him marrying but rather the dead man, who is the legal husband of the woman in question. The Nuer contemplate this as the man lighting the fire of the dead kinsman, a substitute for raising up seeds to him. The foster husband acts as though he were the true husband in the marriage ceremonies and has the same legal rights over the wife as her late husband would have were he alive. The legal husband is not the man and woman living together but rather the ghost of the dead man (Pritchard, 1951). The family that develops out of a ghost marriage is called a ghost family and her children are called *gaat jɔkäh (*meaning children of ghost).

The aim of wife inheritance in Nuer culture was not to satisfy sexual needs or enjoyment, but to produce offspring. That was the core understanding of marriage whether or not in the inheritance of the widow, or marriage for the dead children amongst the Nuer community in South Sudan. For instance, if a man passes on, one of his closest relatives, brother or cousin will inherit his wife. The children, born are considered as offspring of the deceased husband and will bear the deceased husband's name. This is done to keep the name of the deceased alive for ever in the family. In case of the father's death, the eldest son or uncle automatically inherits his step mother or brother's wife. The kind of inheritance is done following the death of the husband and it is done following rituals performed, which end the mourning. From these rituals, the surviving family members start their new life and the surviving spouse starts their life with a new partner. Widow, in particular, must have a man in her mind as her prospective inheritor before the day of the meeting although sometimes family members have a say of who could be the inheritor. When all the processes are over, then, the inheritor starts building his new house, helped by the widow. Among the Nuer, a woman is married not simply by her husband but by his brothers as well, since she is married with the cattle of their common herd.

Naming of Nuer children
Names of Nuer children are received through the male line, and after marriage women reside in the homesteads of their husbands. A newly married woman builds up alliances for her husband's family by maintaining strong relationships with her brothers and sisters who live at her birth place or elsewhere. It is expected that after marriage a woman will bear children for her husband's lineage.

Naming of children are quite meaningful and symbolic in Nuer customs. Nuer names are not mere conventional nominalistic: (a theory that there are no universal essence in reality and that the mind can frame no single concept or inmate corresponding to any inversal or general term), signs or verbal puffs but summarize one's conception of the thing so named. Their names are thought to reveal information about the bearer and describe the circumstances surrounding the birth of the bearer, grandfathers or even explain the experiences of the bearer's parents.

"Nya" meaning girl is the standard prefix used for female names. "Gat" stands for a boy, common prefix used for male names. Although "gat" also means a child. Children are given names to mark historical events. For example, "Nhial" meaning rain for boy and "Nyanhial" for girls are given to child born during the rain. Nhial or Nyanhial is a common name, given to both male and female. When the Missionaries came to Nuer-land, the Nuer have been exposed to Missionaries and giving children Christian names as first names that change the trends of counting back to their generations in terms of social relations. When a young man wants to marry a girl, one of the conditions is to count back lineage relations up to seven for maternal side and eight for paternal to prove that the blood line is distant which can allow the couple to marry. Generally, in the old days, Nuer can easily count up to ten generations of their paternal lineage because they carry these names themselves. Nicknamed: Many Nuer people are nicknamed after their cattle. The boys usually chose the name of their favorite cattle based on the form of its horns and color of the ox. The girls are named after the cows that they milk.

Change of names due to customs
Many Nuer people have been exposed to other traditions and customs such as: Christianity and Islamic some of them carry a Christian and Muslim first names. Although, Islam was rare (unacceptable) in Nuer-land, it was compulsory in schools especially during Islamisation policies in the 1960s and 1970s. Nuer second name is a given name and always in Nuer. The father's given name follows the child's given name, which is then followed by the grandfather's name, and so on. Many Nuer can easily recount ten generations of the paternal lineages

because they carry those names themselves. Similarly, when the Nuer were exposed to the western world, as refugees and further studies, their names change. The first and last name, it is their custom to give their name as their first name followed by their father's name as their middle name and their grandfather's name as their last name. This change of trend would have negative implications for young Nuer people to recount up to ten generations of their paternal lineages because of the gaps created by these new traditions and customs changes.

Gender roles

Like other Nilotic people in South Sudan, gender disparity among the Nuer was common. This was especially true for women whose main duties were to care for children and their husbands. Their responsibilities were limited to home and mainly to the kitchen. By having children, a Nuer woman greatly enhances her power and influence within the lineage of her husband. As the children grow, they take distinct care of their mother interests. Conceivably as many as almost 80% - 100 % percent of Nuer homesteads are polygamous and this contributes to unity between a mother and her children. Nuer woman had to work hard and for long hours to make the household run. In Nuer culture, before the advent of grinding mills, the Nuer had a flat stone call *piil* that was used for grinding grain. The grain was put on this small flat stone for grinding it. *Piil* still even now being used in rural settings in Nuer-land. Grandmothers or the elderly women were experts at this and in many cases, they were the ones who guided young girls in the grinding process (* (appendix 3).

Within the first seven years, the education of respect for elders and sisters begins and will continue without a break until old age. To the ages of seven and fourteen, brothers and senior daughters tell many stories of the clan, some of which contain rules and observations which were broken the consequences which befell those who broke them (Ayayo, 1976). There were some rules, on the other hand, which custom demanded rigid observance by the children: for example, telling the truth, respect for elders, abstaining from theft, non- aggressiveness to younger children and big headedness. Education for the above rules was carried out by parents, senior brothers to youngsters, elder sisters all of whom supervised the teaching of the above rules at the village level.

Traditionally, the Nuer children were told stories by their grandparents. Grandmothers played an important role of socializing girls. From a tender age girl were expected to sleep with their grandmothers in a traditional house called *"duel"* where they were socialized into the communal values and prepared for marriage while the boys on the other hand listened to stories from their grandfathers around a bonfire (*buor*) in the evenings. In addition, women were considered fit to fetch water, collect firewood and cook every day and took care of smaller domestic animals, also protecting crops in the fields against the birds. Collecting wild fruits and was also regarded as women's work. As noted above, agricultural work was fairly equally shared between men and women, with men also responsible for looking after cattle, hunting, physical protection, and warfare. Women had to show high respect towards men. For example, they were expected to kneel down when greeting their husbands and visitors, and usually had to wait until the men had finished with their meals before they take their own food. Men, on the other hand, take the roles of clearing fields, look after life stocks, hunting, fishing and home security. Nuer elders were viewed as custodians of the traditions and customs of the Nuer people and respected by the children.

CHAPTER FIVE:
CULTURE

System of Governance

The Nuer have no centralized political organization. Instead their society is kin-based. The kinship system includes people related both by descent and marriage. When a society is based on relationship, normally it means that family relationships are hereditary through the father's side. The Nuer keep conflict in check by creating alliances that vary according to the context: those who are one's enemy in one situation are one's ally and supporter in another situation because of lineage associations. (Avencino, 2014).

Evans-Pritchard's experience among the Nuer is one of the most important study and most researchers would always refer to it as basic foundation to understand Nuer governing system. Pritchard (1940) asserts that the Nuer people traditionally lack governmental organs, legal institutions, and organized political systems. They are an acephalous state of kinship system that can be understood on the basis of how order is maintained and social relations over wide ranges are established and kept up. Such a community comes out of a product of hard and egalitarian upbringing, remains deeply democratic, and can easily be incited to violence. This turbulent spirit finds any restraint annoying and no man recognizes a superior among them (Pritchard, 1940).

Nuer Traditions and Social Structure

The Nuer traditions, values, and norms are acquired from a strong spiritual traditional belief in the afterlife and a supreme creator (*kuoth*)) with a link to a strong ancestral sprit. This gives the Nuer elders a special social status in society, as they pass petitions to their ancestors in times of need, such as sickness, marriage, harvest and in times of sorrow. These norms and customs also influence the Nuer's marriage and gender relations. Bride selection comes in different forms, which include recommendations from relatives and personal initiations, where men demonstrate their interest in a girl. In this case, girls negotiate with the men who are interested in them until a man wins their favor. Notably, marriage will not take place if there is a blood relationship on either the maternal or paternal side. The Nuer counts the distant of lineages between seven for a girl side and eight for a boy after which they can get involved in marriage.

Ancestral lineages are highly important to the Nuer culture and customs. Their understanding of ancestry through oral history, which has been passed on along many generations, has enabled them to trace their lineages and kept them intact for other Nuer fraternities. The Nuer dowry mainly includes cows, goats and spears which are paid in form of money these days; this is especially common in urban cities where there is no access to cattle. The latter category (goats and spears) may not be paid back in cases of divorce. The marriage ceremony is performed in two stages: it begins with a traditional ceremony, which normally takes place at the bride's home, and this is then followed by a ceremony that takes place in church, the second stage is influenced by Christian and Islamic values and rituals.

The Nuer have a complex structure. Autonomous communities are organized into different clans that follow patrilineal system of decent. This means that membership in a clan is determined by a person's father lineage and property and resources are passed down through male family members. Each Nuer clan is further divided into sub- clans each with its own traditions and customs. Clan lack traditional political authority and are led by religious elders, who play a significant role in settling disputes, decision - making and maintaining the stability of the community. For example, the payment of cattle following a crime such as homicide is mandated by the community's Leopard Skin Chief.

The Nuer system provides no social group with special authority within their clans; every community member participates in decision-making. Despite having influential leaders among them, they do not have powers to enforce their will. The communities make their decisions based on negotiations and consensus. Pritchard and Duany explain this concept in their works: The Nuer political structure described by Pritchard (1956) as a segmentary system whose tendencies of any group work towards fission. Such amalgamation lies at the centre of their political structure. The segmentation of the Nuer into primary, secondary, and tertiary sections is exemplified with the case of different communities and clans within their political system. These fission and fusion tendencies are fundamental principle of the community's social structure (Pritchard, 1956).

Duany in his Text (1992), *Neither Palaces Nor Prisons, the Constitution of Order Among the Nuer,* outlined this segmentary system and aligned groups politically according to their genealogical connections with rules and regulations that govern them. Although the Nuer community members participate in discussion making through consensus, others do not. Nuer women and children do not participate in decision making processes. This is because women are not allowed to play leadership roles by the rules and regulations that govern the Nuer society. In the same manner, children lack any kind of power to make decisions until the time a male child is initiated into adulthood. This was a concern which Pritchard (1940) noted in his inquiry regarding the role of Leopard Skin Chief who acts as a mediator and ritual agent but lacks any kind of political authority to make decisions.

The Nuer concept of "Three Worlds" (Cosmos)
The Nuer traditions is full of collection of undocumented myths that are passed on from the earliest periods down to the current generation, which described Nuer beliefs on their "three worlds": The world of living (*rol-tekä)*; world of the waiting dead (*rol-liepä –jɔkni*) and world of the dead (*rol-jɔkni).* The Nuer culture shows the patterns of behaviors that led to the study of life after death and creation that explains the understanding toward the Nuer philosophy. According to Nuer philosophy, the, three worlds exist in the cosmos and all of them are interconnected. These worlds have a direct impact to their beliefs and the way they conduct their lives. The communication between the three habits had been possible through the means of dreams. The story of life, death and burial ceremonies still make a satisfactory tune in Nuer community. The Nuer first world is the current living world (*rol-tekä*) which is transitioning to another world is occurring. This is the place where the human beings (Nuer) live. The three worlds are believed to be lively in a sense that they still transmit information

from one world to another through dreams. It was these dreams that were used as a mean of communication from one person to another. The other important aspect of the worlds is the invisible lines that make them to communicate and transmit information across their worlds.

Traditionally, Nuer considers old people who were dead long ago still alive in glittery heaven which they called (world of the waiting dead (*rol-liepä –jɔkni).* Because of this, when there is sickness that befalls the family; Nuer community elders always beckon the spirit of the deceased to come for help. Rituals and sacrifices are offered and the spirit of the dead responds. When elders beckon the spirit, they do not look down on earth where the dead is buried, instead, they face the sky and speak to the dead person whom they believe is in the world of the waiting dead. This waiting world, is said to be situated in the shiny heaven above. Once a person dies, the body goes back to the earth and the Soul goes to the world of the waiting dead. These people are considered like Saints who have been doing good things on earth. Elderly people who died because of old age, the Nuer believed that they are closer to God and are always consulted when the family is encountered with illnesses and death. They are the ones being remembered when someone is giving something to drink or eat; small part of it will be poured or dropped to the group. This is giving them some share of food or drink. They live together with the gods in the sky. It is this world where curse is observed even at this age that when an old man who is alive curse you, the effect of the curse will be felt by the person on earth (ground). Nuer also think that there is life in the shiny heaven and that symbolism was represented by the story of a three stars seen following each other in line. The story represents one person taking the cow by the rope, followed by the one helping and a dog after them. This depicts a practical situation perceived on earth with the Nuer cattle herders. In adding, the Nuer believe that elders who died are there in heaven.

There are understandings that impacted the way Nuer give sacrifices and summoned the dead to respond on the family crisis. When a person dies, the body will go back to the soil and soul will separate. People who died as sinners or who have been committing crimes either through magic or homicide, they will be kept in *rol jɔkni.* When the family faces crisis these dead people are not called upon for help. The world of the dead or *rol jɔkni* is believed to be situated under the ground and this is the place where those people who did evil things dwell. Those who have been killing people unjustly either through magic or intentionally are kept in this place. They are also communicating to people with bad dreams that talk of revenge and killings. This group of people is not mentioned when elders are giving sacrifices and they are ignored and forgotten once they are dead. A living testimony cited by Kim (2017), revealed that when men dig wells, the dead are always complaining of cutting the ropes of their goats in a place called *Thornhom* in *Ganyliel* Town of *Panyijiar* County in Western Upper Nile State. The above place of that incident, is said to be an open ground where the men and women of different ages mysteriously disappeared while they were playing traditional dance at night. It is believed that there is a component within the community who state that there is connection between the spiritual leaders and the way the Stars, Moon and the Sun and heavenly bodies are linked to the Nuer social life.

Two worlds of the three: (world of the waiting dead and world of the dead), where people who are dead should go to according to Nuer beliefs: Those who died with no crimes will live in shiny heaven which they called world of the waiting dead (*rol-liepä –jɔkni*). The second group goes to the world of the dead (*rol jɔkni)*, believed to be situated under the ground and this is the place where those people who have done evil things reside. The sense of spirituality and belief in divine power is traditionally embedded in Nuer culture. For instance, the Nuer people traditionally believed in the afterlife, and they still see their ancestral sprits as holy messengers that transmit their supplications to a divine power in heaven in their time of need. Therefore, it was no wonder when Christianity with its philosophy of life after death was introduced by the missionaries, it echoed with Nuer traditions and beliefs. Christianity then influenced the Nuer's religious practices and beliefs, particularly those living in towns and urban cities.

Death and burial ceremonies
Death is a big issue among the Nuer and always a cause for the death is involved. It marks the beginning of an elaborate rite of passage for both the dead person and his living families. At death, the body is deposed off in a highly respected manner with all ceremonies that suit it. The burial is a whole community affair where relatives and friends come from far and wide to wail, mourn and to comfort the family of the deceased. Traditionally, when an old person died, the burial was immediate, and if one dies in permanent settlement the remains is laid to rest in his hut. A hole is dug and the deceased insert in the hole with face to the east. I asked one elder why east? It is recorded that "all good things come from the east (sunrise) and bad things go with sunset" (*kuonychäŋ*). Although this is no longer practiced, the body of the deceased is still buried within the homestead and the individual's hut remains unoccupied to erode over time. In the urban settings however, if someone dies away from home, the body is returned to their homestead for burial. It is imperative that even those Nuer who live in distant cities be brought back to their homestead for burial out of their own house. During and after funerals, Nuer consume large amounts of meat, beer, and white stuffs and socialize with friends and relatives. Funerals last for several days depending on the circumstance a person died. Once the deceased is buried the process of cleansing starts.

The Nuer mourning (*par*) ceremony is a unique, elaborate and dramatic ceremony that symbolizes the departure of a loved one is still widely practiced among the Nuer society. The relationship between the dead and their living relatives is expressed most fully in the ritual of sacrifice. The ritual of sacrifice consists of various elements, which include the sanctification of the animal to be sacrificed, the slaughtering and the offering of the animal and the distribution of meat among the living members of the lineage. If the living dead are offended, the head of the household must seek help from specialist diviners on what to do. The concept of the living dead was significant because it served as a moral limit on the people still living, averting them from mistreating those who would otherwise have been helpless in the absence of their dead relatives, mostly children left behind. After the burial an expression of grief testimonies, there is a period of feasting and celebration. Normally, the brother or close relative of the deceased presides over the ritual process. This signifies the end of person's lifetime on earth when a new homestead is yet to be founded. People who come for funerals are housed around the compound of the deceased, where he or she is buried. It is imperative that even those Nuer who live in diaspora and distant cities are brought back to their homestead for burial.

Rituals (ceremonies) are performed in certain, fixed ways to reflect how a particular death occurred, the good deeds of the deceased, and the way the ancestors had performed are linked up in the ceremonies. The Nuer have many ceremonies connected with death, burials, funerals, inheritance, and the living dead. The belief in the spirits of the dead is common and widespread among the Nuer. There are key components of culture, largely influencing Nuer behaviour, which are passed on from one generation to the other, of course with modifications. Culture influences people apparently because it provides them with an identity and a worldview through which they interpret their universe. In Nuer culture, belief in the spirits of the dead provides a basis for most of the practices that take place from the time one dies to the end of the mourning period. Spirits of the dead are feared since, if one does not comply with the customs, then he/she is haunted by them. A burial ceremony has to be performed at even a drowned person's home, he answered that if the ceremonies were not done, "the spirits of the dead would haunt the people, claiming they were ignored" (Ojijo 2012).

The Nuer believe that a human being is made up of visible - the body (*puony*) and invisible parts (*yie*). The union of the two parts forms Nuer human life. At death the body perishes, but *yie* becomes the spirit. The spirit recalls the individual identity, but develops more intelligent and powerful than in the previous world. The spirit becomes demon (*joh*) in their spiritual form though, not separated from their clans. The above Nuer beliefs lead to certain practices during and after the mourning period of the dead which the Nuer accords due respect with the consequence that among other things, dead bodies must be disposed of in a dignified and respectful manner, with all ceremonies that suit it. Bodies are buried homesteads, graves protected from digging of wild animals such as hyenas for several days after the burial. Other communal places for burial included; near water watercourses, banks of rivers, etc. The Nuer believe that there is always a cause for the death. A person who dies of old age is thought to have been called by the ancestors to join them for more duties because they believe that spiritual beings are more powerful than the living. The Nuer traditionally believed in life after death and a supreme creator, whom they call *kuoth*. Most Nuer also hold view of death and the afterlife influenced by their participation in Christian and Islamic religions due to modernization and change.

The Nuer were once independent before the coming of colonizers. They had control and freedom over their own politically defined world which they called *Rol Naath*. This was a homogenous state with social hierarchy with temporal base, like events relevance to appropriate time and person, to do the tasks such as that of the British Common Laws. They had their own regular institutions of enforcing traditional rules and regulations. Their social control was maintained through the systematic application of "segmentary" organized society. This means that the Nuer had no written 'laws' in the past. They had recognized standards for the control of their human relationships. The only institutions that existed and respected among the Nuer was that of the Leopard Skin Chief discussed in the next section, whose duties were settlement of feuds; concerned with the spiritual welfare of a killer as an individual and acts as mediator between conflicting parties and the community elders who act as custodians in the society. The government appointed chiefs came later in 1930s and play roles after British intervention that transformed the Nuer egalitarian system of governance.

Evolution on Nuer political System

Nuer courts were established under the Chief's Courts Ordinance 1931 which was also applied to other Southern Provinces of the Sudan: the Bahr el Ghazal, Equatoria, and the Upper Nile. It was this time a system of law in Nuer segmentary society was in a state of evolution. This evolutionary process was rooted in the traditional methods of controlling the acts of individuals and groups, none of which methods was rigid. The evolution had also been affected by the decision made in the courts, often by the direct intervention of British Administrators who had neither known nor understood the principles involved. They made decisions without appreciating that Nuer ideas of justice are often different from that of their own (Howell, 2018). It was because of these insensitivities that it took a longer time for the Nuer to submit to British District Commissioner's judgments which they viewed as alien.

The British entered Sudan in the late 18th century and installed their policies on the Sudanese people as well as among the Nuer, represented by Administrators and District Commissioners. Many researchers such as Hutchinson (1996), have found that the Nuer had no chiefs or kings among them, until 1930 when few government chiefs were appointed, neither out of their effectiveness as local leaders nor loyalty as government agents, encouraged British Administrator's confidence. As a result, semblance of a wider political order existed based more on shifting pattern of intercommunity alliance and feuding than the few labors of British administrators at the time, became more concern on how to improve the Nuer egalitarian system based on a combination of kinship and residency affiliations, loosely divided into major, territorial groupings (Hutchinson, 1996). The British used a combination of diplomacy and swift territorial occupation, following its victory over the Khalifa in September 1898. British key interest in Southern Sudan during that period was strategic: first, to occupy the South in order to control the Nile Basin. Other factors including economies and development of the people who lived in the region were of no importance (Alier, 2003).

After the end of Second World War, nationalists demands for independence increased led by the Graduate. Congress in the north started pressing administration to end "Southern Policy". The Civil Secretary, Sir Douglas Newbold, responded in 1944 with a statement of new policy in the South, which was to act upon the fact that people of Southern Sudan are distinctively African and Negroid and that the government duty to them was to push ahead with economic and educational development programs that would equip them to stand up for themselves in the future. Changes happened anyway, that led to reversal of "Southern Policy", despite resistance mounted by Southern people including the Nuer. For this cause, Nuer people met the threat of repression with violence and resistance that accounts for their backwardness in human development. I provide a brief background on some of the Nuer leaders of resistance which serve to illustrate the extent to which either individually or collectively made a lasting contribution to the cause of their freedom as a people.

The practical historians of the Nuer society accounts that: the Nuer hero who had called his "dog" *Kac-lorä* (nonsense/action) was a man called Dhiew Dieng from Lɔu Nuer. He was regarded by the British Colonial Administration as double agent both loyal to the Prophet Guɛk Ngundɛŋ and the Government (*Turuk)* at the same time. His dog's name was twisted as an abusive to British administrators by those Nuer who sought the position from *Turuk* after the death of Prophet Guɛk Ngundɛng from Lɔu Nuer. After the Nuer settlement between 1929 and 1931 Dhiew was arrested by the colonial authority and was kept as political detainee along with Reath Ngundɛng and Weituor Beah (Bei) in Malakal where other Nuer leaders were kept by the same authority: Char Koryom, Puok Kerjiok, Gatluak Nyak Gok from Nyuong and Prophet Dual Diu from Gaawäär-Nuer. The main reason leading to the arrest of Nuer chiefs and Prophets according to traditional source was an accusation leveled by '*Guɛt Thiech'* who was the appointed chief by British (*Turuk)* from Lou Nuer. His conspiracy led to the death of Guɛk Ngundɛng and subsequent political character assassination of other traditional leaders (*rueec*) such as Dhiew Dieng, Rɛath Ngundɛng, Weituor Bei, Char Koryom, Puok Kerjiok and Dual Diu mentioned above. However, Chuol Weng and Gatkek Jiek, '*aka'* Kuel Jiek who killed Fergusson DC of western Nuer earlier in 1927 were betrayed by Wuon Kuoth who had served as a chief of *Turuk* in Nyuong Nuer, while Gatluak Nyak who was survivor of war which he fought against the British alongside the Prophet Kulang Ket was killed earlier in 1925 by Awaraquay (Fergusson) the western Nuer DC.

The British colonial hostilities against the Nuer Prophet Ling Puot's homestead in Jagei Nuer was also reported. Buom Diew from Dok Nuer who joined Kulang Ket and Gatluak Nyak had escaped to Gaawäär during that war (1927). The DC Fergusson (*Warakuei*) killed Kulang Ket using the territories of Chaath-hok Bang and his friends. The report indicates that Chaath- hok Bang had earlier on buried Kulang Ket alive. It is said that Kulang Ket cursed both Chaath-hok Bang and his friend Fergusson during his brutal murdered. Afterwards, Warakuei was killed in 1927 in Dor Nyuong by Gatkek Jiek *(*Kuel Jiek), and Chaath-hok Bang who had buried the Prophet Kulang Ket alive was killed by an elephant during the hunting raid in the forest of Nyuong in 1930. If this narrative was correct, then, the spirit of the Prophet Kulang Ket could be explained in Nuer religious understandings to have had punished his culprits and died in the same way he was brutally killed because of his curse to them.

Figure n₄4 7 Body of Prophet Guɛk Ngundɛŋ hanged on the Tree of Bad Things (*kuel jiäkni*).

Image adapted with permission from Douglass Johnson's Nuer Prophets.

As the hostilities against the Nuer Prophets continued, the report further states that Ferry Corriat, the DC of central Nuer, avenged the murder of DC Fergusson by killing Guek Ngundɛng hanging his body on the tree in Wei-Deang (I (Figure no: 4 above). ,uch a suicidal killing of Nuer Prophet Guɛk Ngundɛng carried out by the British forces falls among the negative actions in Nuer society. This British action of hanging the body on the tree resulted in severe violent resistance all over the Nuerland.

In addition to these developments and resistant of *turuk* policies in Nuer Nation, a man from western Nuer named Tang Kuany had mobilized some Western Nuer labors for Saayid Abdularahman El Mahdi's estate in Khartoum and advocated to convert them to Islam. This kind of behaviour annoyed the Western Nuer men during the second half of the twentieth century and led to his death in Malakal in 1956. Many Nuer traditional and spiritual leaders were praised and highly appreciated for resisting colonial policies and these leaders were viewed as genuine ones who stood and spoke on behalf of their people. However, some Nuer leaders, especially Ngundɛng Bong, Chaath-hok Bang, and Wuon Kuoth Guɛt Thiech were considered as betrayers.

 Guɛt Thiech was accused by betraying Guɛk Ngundɛng leading to his death in February 1927. Though, other traditional sources indicate that Guɛt was not involved directly, but it was Lam Tuthiang, Biɛl Pɛat from Lɔu Nuer and Deng Malual from Nyarraweng Dinka who accompanied the British forces to Wei Deang. Moreover, Tang Kuany was accused by the Nuer as traitor who collaborate with colonials' systems. Nuäär cruelly betrayed the central Nuer to the Turco-Egyptian' slavers. Chaath –hok Bang was responsible for the murder of western Nuer leader Kulang Ket and he was considered as a traitorous intermediary to Captain Fergusson. And that Wuon Kuoth had betrayed his own cousin Gatkek Jiek who was hanged with Chuol Weng in Dor Nyuoŋ in 1930 by Percy Corriat. He did this for the sake of gaining a chieftaincy position the report added.

However, it was likely that the Nuer did not understand nor differentiate the roles of the newly appointed government chiefs at that time and therefore, came to conclusions without knowing why the government appointed chiefs might have behaved in the ways they acted to support the *Turuk* (government) rather than being betrayers. The Nuer however, were by no means one people with a set of coordinated plans all over the Nuer Nation for resisting colonial administration and were also united at war with their neighbors. This perhaps, could be one of the reasons that made British DCs' intervention to address this culture of violence administratively leading to changes on Nuer political systems.

The role of Leopard Skin Chief
The Nuer settled feuds through the Leopard Skin Chief. Research reveals that this functionary position has spiritual powers to persuade parties in conflict. Though he does not have authority to make decision regarding the disputes, based on Nuer traditions, Leopard Skin Chief has sacred association with the earth - *mun*. This association gives the chief certain ritual powers in relation to it, including the power to bless or curse. However, it should be noted that such powers of uttering curses do not enable him to wield great authority.

Practically, the Nuer people have the traditional system of authority to enforce decisions through dialogue. Such authority is summoned when the need to resolve disputes between the warring parties arise. The main actor in this institution is Leopard Skin Chief (*kuär twac*). According to Nuer customs, when disputes between close relatives arise, most of the community members are required to be unbiased in managing the dispute. But, when dispute arises between members of distant clans or sections, each disputant can call on large sections of his clan for support. This makes the conflict high enough that people are willing to negotiate rather than escalates tensions and risk violence or even murder.

Photo by: Nhial Gai Wuor.

This practice helps avoid *Nueer* (contamination), which may lead to death. By this ritual, the Leopard Skin Chief has thus intervened to stop the escalation of violence. It is important to note that the Leopard Skin Chief is not a chief in the technical sense. He gives summons when the community expects the costs of a violent act to be too costly. In an egalitarian structure such as Nuer, the Leopard Skin Chief does not dictate a resolution, and he cannot enforce an agreement. He does not have political or executive authority to compel parties in conflicts to abide by the decision to pay compensation. Instead, he is a dispute mediator who works as an impartial middleman to negotiate a resolution after slaying an animal in atonement. His office is spiritual and the symbol of his office is a spear and a leopard skin. The office is hereditarily held by a priestly clan. Despite these limitations, Leopard Skin Chief is respected by the Nuer as a person who only has moral force to make the parties in a conflict to comply and to reach a consensus through dialogue and performs rituals.

Leopard Skin Chief performs all types of rituals including oath taking after the conflicts are resolved. The home of Leopard Skin Chief is sacred and any offender who seeks refuge in his residence is spared by the offended. The Nuer believe that the role of Leopard Skin Chief is to offer spiritual wisdom of moderate between the spiritual world and humanity. In Nuer customs, if someone is killed or murdered, it is the responsibility of the victim's kin to seek justice to avoid escalation of violence. Before the ritual process is completed, the slayer may neither eat nor drink. If he fears vengeance, as is normally the case, he remains at the chief's home. The preceding few months after the incident, the Leopard Skin Chief engages with the slayer's kin to find out if they are prepared to compensate the aggrieved to avoid a feud. During this period, neither party may eat or drink from the same vessel. According to Nuer customs, going against this instruction may cause misfortune such as the slayer being haunted by the blood of the late. After completing the negotiation process, it is the chief's duty to collect the cattle and take them to the dead man's home. While there, Leopard Skin Chief performs various sacrifices to cleanse the killer.

Recent changes in Nuer administrative set up in the institutions have created doubts about the roles of Leopard Skin Chief within the Nuer society. For example, during Christmas pastoral visit in 2021 to Akobo County – Dirror Payam, in a meeting held with Leopard Skin Chief named Kun Yai, it is recorded that "this institution of Leopard Skin Chief is no longer respected as it used to be in the past". Previously when a man has killed another person, he must at once go to a Leopard Skin Chief's home, who would perform the ritual of cleansing by pricking his finger to allow his blood to flow and also for his safety. But at present, is no longer the case. Nowadays, this function is done by the local authority mainly the Area Commanders contrary to the Nuer customs. The Leopard Skin Chief does no longer intervene to stop the escalation of violence between the warring parties. This institution and its functionaries are no longer relevant. Presently, the Leopard Skin Chief is only called in as ritual agent to perform sacrifices and oath taking.

The other important actor in Nuer governing system with adverse effects is the government appointed Chiefs - *Kuär Biey (Kuär Buok.)*. These leaders were first appointed by the British administrators in 1930s. Since then, government-appointed chiefs are members of the Nuer Customary Law Courts. They decide on criminal and civil cases. Examples of societal wrongs and the compensations these chiefs can force include; adultery (*dhoom)*, for which the offender pays fines (*ruɔk ciek)* of six heads of cattle to the husband of the women involved in the adultery. Of these six head of cattle, five are considered to be direct compensation for the injury caused to the husband and the sixth cow i.e. for "the sleeping–skin" known as ("*yang koli*") which has a religious significance. *Yang koli* (sleeping skin) is symbolic marital relations. In this connection, a man does not sleep with his wife after she has had inter-course with another man, she is considered to be in state of impurity and a return to conjugal relations will bring misfortune to them unless the process of compensation is completed.

Similarly, an individual who elopes with a girl or commits illicit sexual offence with an unmarried girl, pays *ruok* or *ruol ciokni* of three cows to the girl's father. In addition, the chief's functions are mediation in accidental death and physical injuries cases. Such incidents call for payment (*cut)* to the victim's parents. The introduction of customary courts initiated by the government in 1930s into the Nuer society did not contradict the role of the Leopard Skin Chief. Cases that require oath taking are referred to the spiritual actor before the government chief's court makes final decisions.

Photo by: Gabriel Gai Riam

It is to be noted that Nuer traditional institutions and social behaviour have undergone radical changes as a result of the prolonged civil war and other factors. The mechanism of the Nuer traditional systems outlined above is so much affected. For instance, the Nuer youth who are well armed do not listen nor respect their chiefs nowadays, leave alone the soldiers who always intimidate traditional chiefs. As such, chiefs and other traditional leaders lost influence over their subjects.

These contextual presentations have provided an in-depth exploratory study of the Nuer cultural development and the community's values. The Nuer culture highlighted how tribal egalitarian societies such as the Nuer adapted to their environments and settled disputes without formal leadership. They had recognized principles for the control of their relationships, though these were maintained by consents and less legal. However, considering the history of Nuer people, it is difficult for them to engage with the larger world due to social changes and developments the global community and the virtual world bring about.

Nuer language (*Thok Naath*)
Nuer people are rich in culture and language like any society where languages are being considered as mechanism of communications. Nuer were aware that they live in a world where Nations transfer values, norms and equality in this shared world. Nuer language/Thok Naath belongs to the Nilo-Saharan language group. Nuer origin traditions, archaeological evidence, and discourses of otherness all indicate that the river-Lake Nilotes of Sudd began to distinguish among the ethnic groupings that exist today far more recently than scholars who use glottochronology have suggested on the basis of linguistic differentiation.

Numerous specialists who have worked in the Sudd have tried to date local processes of ethno-genesis with essentially the same style of glottochronology that celebrated historical-linguists to all of Nilotic East Africa and they have produced similarly ancient dates by taking language as cognate with ethnicity. These techniques were first applied to River-Lake Nilotic languages dated the "ancient divergence" between Proto-Luo (the common ancestor of *Dhø cøllø, Dhòk Anywaa, Dhi päri, Dholuo* among others now spoken to the north of the Sudd and Sudd-centered Proto-Dinka-Nuer to 335 B.C.E (Before Christian Epoch: used when referring before the birth of Jesus Christ when the Christian calendar begins counting the years). Such studies also calculated that the "Dinka" (*thuɔŋjäŋ*) line of herders diverged from "Nuer" (*thok naath*) a bit later, around 85 C.E (Common Era), (Raymond, 1985). Johnson (1997) subsequently argued for higher rates of the cognation taken to mark closeness, and hence recency of dating, among these languages than his predecessors had detected. Those who accept glottochronology's logarithmic premises would suggest that *thuɔŋjäŋ* and *thok naath* diverged even more recently around the tenth century (Johnson, 1997). However, even this more recent date comes several centuries before the first teeth-exactors identified in the northern Sudd and suggests that modern-day markers to differentiate between dry-side herders (*Nuer* and *Jiëëŋ*) and riverine cultivators (*Collo Luo*, and *Anywaa*) emerged along a different historical trajectory.

As point of entry to Nuer Language, let us first highlight the general language situation between the Nuer and their neighbours because this may enable us understand the closeness of Nilotic peoples in the past and present. The Nilotic languages cover over forty related languages and dialects spoken by many people in six countries mostly in East Africa: the South Sudan, Uganda, Ethiopia, Kenya and Tanzania (Prah, 2000). The purpose of listing these languages is to identify and classify languages according to families and related mutually intelligible clusters. This is a convenient way to represent them in terms of the family tree model used by historical linguists. So that this will allow one to show how closely Nuer language is related to other Nilotic languages spoken in the past even at the present are related to one another. This will answer part of the question: where did the Nuer come from? And it will also show the reader how far each has diverged from others as a result of historical changes and more importantly, will clarify Nuer cultural narrative with their neighbors in the next subsection. Nilotic languages of Africa are classified into three distinct linguistic groups as follows: (1) Niger-Kordofanian (including Bantu languages), (2) Nilo-Saharan including: (Sudanic and Nilotic languages) and (3) Afro-Asiatic family (Cushitic, Somali and Galla). The Nilotic branch is further divided up into three sub-branches: Western Nilotic (WN), Eastern Nilotic (EN) and Southern Nilotic (SN) (Prah, 2000) but this text is mainly concerned about Western Nilotic from which the Nuer people are grouped as shown in Table 7.1 below.

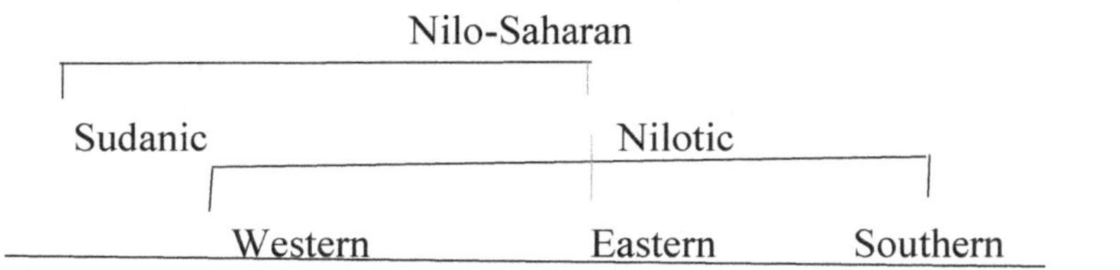

Table 7.1:

Western, Eastern and Southern Languages
The specific languages found in these families are shown in Table 7. 2 below. The languages of the Western Nilotic which include Dinka, Nuer, Shilluk and the Dholuo of Kenya have the largest number of speakers (1973 and 1989 censuses). These similarities would help the reader to follow any discussion on cultural relations between Nuer and other ethnic communities. The presupposition is that since these languages originated from a common proto language, they would share at least some common linguistic features. The idea is that the closer a group of languages, the more features they share and probably the more intelligible they are to each other.

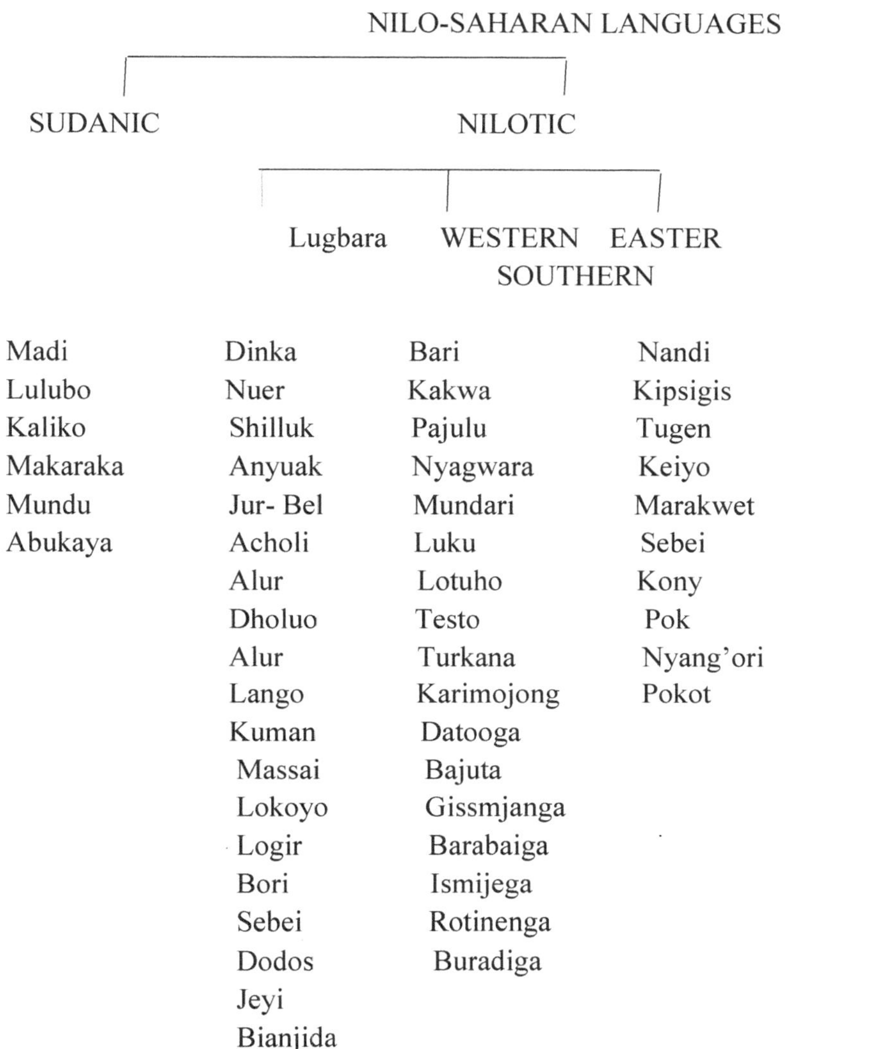

Table 8 7: Nilo Saharan Languages (Prah, 2000)

As Johnson (2015) describes in South Sudan, as in Uganda, some of the regional political divisions have been labelled in broadly ethnic terms, as in Equatoria Vs "Nilotic" (South Sudan) or Bantu of the South Vs "Nilotic" of North (Uganda). The word "Nilotic" does not cover the same groups in each country. Whereas the Nilotic in South Sudan is generally understood to mean the western Nilotic speaking Dinka and Nuer, it is not colloquially applied to this way to the western Nilotic –speaking Acholi or Pari of Equatoria. And while in Uganda the so called "Nilotic" do include the Acholi and Lango of the North, they also include such non-western Nilotic peoples as the Lugbara of West Nile.

In Ethiopia too, the word "Nilotic" is applied to anyone in the southern lowlands, irrespective of their native language. Thus, the term "Nilotic" can sometimes be very confusing if not misleading. However, the study of history is the search for real connections, for real origins and it can be a way to expand beyond parochial concern, (Johnson, 2015). As noted in the above Table, Nilotic languages and their connection give a clear understanding that western Nilotic are very similar and linked to the rest of African continent.

Tangible and intangible culture
Cattle have historically been, and still remain, the highest symbolic, religious and economic value to the Nuer people of South Sudan. Cattle are particularly important in their role as bride wealth, where they are given by a husband's lineage to his wife's lineage. This exchange of cattle ensures that the children will be considered to belong to the husband's lineage. The classic Nuer institution of ghost marriage, in which a man can "father" child after his death, is based on this characterization of relations of kinship and descent by cattle exchange. Usually, when marriage negotiations are done, cows are given to the wife's patrilineage to enable the male children of that patrilineage to marry and thereby ensure the continuity of her patrilineage. An infertile woman can even take a wife of her own, whose children, biologically fathered by men from other unions, then become members of her patrilineage, and she is legally and culturally their father, allowing her metaphorically participate in reproduction.

It is important to note how intangible cultural heritage (ICH) such as that of the Nuer is perceived globally nowadays. For example, UNESCO'S Convention for the safeguarding of the intangible culture heritage of various communities was adopted by the UNESCO General Conference on October 17th 2003. The idea of intangible culture heritage was ratified at a convention in 2006 by 178 member states including South Sudan in March 2016 (UNESCO, 2003). The goal is to invite countries to care about and look after the ICH present on their territories.

Intangible cultural heritage is living expressions inherited from peoples' ancestors and passed on to their descendants, such as "oral traditions, performing arts, social practices, rituals, events, knowledge and practices concerning nature and the universe or the knowledge and skills to produce traditional crafts. Categories of intangible cultural heritage include oral traditions and expression like proverbs, riddles, tales, legends, myths, epic songs and poems, charms, chants, songs and more. Performing arts can include music, dance and theatre, pantomime, songs and other forms of artistic expression that are passed down from generation to generation.

Social practices like rituals and festive events including initiation rites, burial ceremonies, seasonal carnivals and harvest celebrations form part of intangible heritage. Other aspects include knowledge and practices concerning nature and the universe such as knowhow and skills that communities have developed by interacting with their natural environment, and may be expressed through language, memories, spirituality or worldviews.

Traditional methods of architecture, agriculture, cattle breeding, and cuisine are among the related elements. Nuer traditional craftsmanship refers to the skills and knowledge involved in craftsmanship than the products themselves include pottery, woodwork, jewelry and precious stones; embroidery, carpet weaving, musical instrument production, weaving and fabric production. These are most categories of intangible culture heritage practiced in Nuer society (s (see appendix 3).

Sample of food and domestic articles
Typical foods eaten by the Nuer community include: beef (*riiŋ*), goat, cow's milk, fish and sorghum in one of three forms of foods: "kọp" finely ground, handled until balled and boiled, "*nup*" ground, lightly balled and boiled to a solid porridge the name comes from Arabic word (steer), and kisira (Yɔtyɔt) (Arabic word), a large, pancake-like yeast-risen flatbread and *Kuän Naath* (food of the people). Pumpkins (*kolong/monyjo*), beans (*Ngoar*) etc. The Nuer people are characterized as agro-pastoralists. They grow vegetables as grains such as millet.

Nuer diets are composed primarily of milk, fish, vegetables, and grain. Cow beef is rarely eaten only on special occasions such as after sacrifice. Fishing and growing of vegetables, and grain such as millet. (Sorghum and maize) are common among the Nuer. Their lifestyle is semi-nomadic, moving from place to place with their cattle in search of water and pasture. During the dry seasons, they live along the Nile River and streams and in the dry seasons they migrate to permanent villages on higher ground. This lifestyle shapes their cultural values which emphasize independence self-reliance and strong community bonds. The Nuer have strong oral tradition and place great importance on story-telling, music and dance as ways of preserving their cultural heritage.

Ornaments and value of age-sets (*riic*)
Nuer people, like other Nilotic peoples of South Sudan, are inseparable from their history and intangible culture heritage. The Nuer share cultures such as naming, food, rituals, and dispute resolution mechanisms with Dinka, Anyuak and *cøllø*. The Nuer receive facial markings as part of their initiation into adulthood which they called (*gäri*), dance, arts and drama ceremonies, knowledge and practices concerning nature and the universe and skills to produce tradition crafts, all of which have been and are still being profoundly influenced by their environments.

The age-sets among the Nuer are an institution in the larger clan that have the same open and closed periods. These ages set system gives Nuer society the pride of grouping generation after generation. Each section of the Nuer community has its own age-set organization. Adjacent clan(s) co-ordinate their sets in periods and nomenclature, so that communities in western, eastern, and central Nuer fall into three divisions in this respect. When an individual travels from one area to another in the Nuer land, they can easily perceive their age mate. Despite the clarity of these sets and the ease of identifying them, their naming varies from region to region. Each of the four sections in Nuer land, that is, Western, Central, *Jikäny* and *Lou* Nuer have different names for different age sets. With exception of those age–sets that were initiated and named before their migration from west to eastern Nile (*kiir käny chäng*). The Nuer do not have female age-set. Except those who dance together are considered. At times they are enrolled into into their husbands' age set.

Nuer people retain such knowledge about their particular families because they find it inherently meaningful to them, they also mark persons in other ways that make their collective knowledge of the past more useful to other people such like researchers. These corporate naming for age sets practices revolves around what researchers generally called "age-sets" (*ric*) which Stringham (2016) translates as "marriageability-sets". This conveys the primary purpose among the Nuer society. Age sets are gender-specific cohorts of male peers initiated at the same time by having a distinctive mark – six parallel horizontal lines (*gäär*) scarified across their foreheads. Each age - set is given a collective name such as "White-Hearts" (*Boi-loc*) referred to the symptoms of cattle lung sickness that devastated Nuer herds in the early 1860s, or "Sudan" for those initiated during the independence of Sudan in 1956 (Stringham, 2016). The pattern of Nuer scarification varies within specific subgroups. The most common initiation pattern among males consists of six parallel horizontal lines which are cut across the forehead with a special traditionally disinfected knife (*ŋom*), often with a dip in the lines above the nose. Spotted patterns are also common especially among the Bul of western and eastern Lɔu and Janay Nuer and among their females.

 Each community has an expert whose privilege is to set initiation periods and name each set. This expert performs the ritual to each set while calling on the special relationship with cattle, seen as the ritual is referred to as *gäär* (refer to the previous part). He opens and closes initiation periods in his own clan/community. The gap between age sets is between three to four years. Once a set is opened, each village and clan initiate its boys as is necessary. The formality of initiation among the Nuer does not require formal education or moral training, only through observation. An elder from the Nuer community, told me that sometimes a young person (s) from an expert lineage observes the performance of this rite of initiation in preparation for eventual takeover an experience which I personally observed and experienced.

In Nuer culture, an uninitiated young man is prohibited from eating some parts of a cow's meat such as ribs or any animal's ribs, for that matter. Such prime cuts *kau* are preserved for the young initiated male persons as a prize for passing these corporates ritual ceremony. This custom is common throughout the Nuerland. The final stage of an individual's life is arrived until the time he passed on, and even then, he is ritually incorporated into the wider family of both the living and the dead. Which anthropologically, the Nuer believe that the dead are still alive spiritually among them; that's why the Nuer marries for a dead person and that the children born by a widow after husband died belongs to the dead man.The dead person is considered to have rights that the living relatives must preserve.

Although, these practices exist in some Nilotic societies, the Nuer take them a bit more spiritually. They believe the same way God made first man, it is their responsibility to make and transform an individual into a social entity, deeply rooted to the religious transaction. A Nuer individual only becomes complete if he is linked to others in the society to whom he carries a responsibility. When he experienced an individual suffering, it does not record as such; rather, as part of a corporate entity. The same applies to his happiness; he rejoices with his kinsmen; neighbor and his relatives be they dead or alive. When he marries, he does so not as an island but as a part of his community, and his wife, too, belongs to their entire community. This premise, however, does not apply to the sexual obligations to the husband, which are specific to him alone. Besides, his children, despite bearing his name, belong to the corporate body of the tribe.

Responsibility to the community
This assumption implies that whatever happens to the individual affects his entire clan and anything that affects the clan has a bearing on the individual person. Some scholars, such as Mbiti agree with this Nuer school of thought, asserting that the African individual lives by the principle of: 'I am, because we are; and since we are, therefore I am' (Mbiti, 1969). This is a cardinal point in understanding the Nuer view of an individual person, especially with regards to his responsibilities and accountability. The concept of responsibility: it is participating in society, being part of institutions and practices, and finding ourselves in positions of responsibility with obligations to others and duties to be performed. These are not detractions from the good life but an essential part of its nature (Solomon and Clancy, 2004).

Any Nuer participating in society's undertaking holds some responsibility. They must be accountable for their duties, obligations, whatever authorities they have been assigned. This accountability in Nuer context presents itself in regards to the spiritual world and the kinship community which explains that equality is related to the Nuer concept and accountability is collective social responsibility. It holds individuals who have committed crimes responsible for their actions and allows the same principle to extend universality, creating a particular kind of moral environment for each other. In this sense of relationship, the Nuer commitment to their social system of reciprocal accountability gives incentives to work out the fuller exegesis of their system of regulatory principle. It's this system of justice and equality that gives the Nuer the moral compass to call themselves *Naath,* a differentiating feature from other ethnic communities. In other texts, Riam (2022), has explained the terms *Naath* and Nuer exhaustively in his text; entitled *Christian-Muslim Relations in Sudan: A study of the relationship between Church and State*. The same concept has been discussed by Kim (2017): *The Discourse on the Origin of the terms Naath and Nuer.*

Comparatively, Turaki (2006), affirms that similar to Nuer individual person, another African man is not to be responsible for their action alone, as they are considered an extension of the spirit world; the corporate family and tribe. Together, these entities must share responsibilities and blames for what has happened. This community of kinsfolk can only survive if it has good relationships with both the natural and spiritual world (Turaki, 2006). Thus, a community of kinsfolk pursues harmony with world around it; strives for a meaning with the spiritual world, goes after the mystical and spiritual powers to survive and maintains itself for its own security.

Here, an illustration of the Nuer perception of corporate responsibility is presented. For example, forgiveness (*pälikä* – *Pälikä)* means forgiveness. It demands a dramatic public confession between communities or individuals. *Pälikä* in its highly public character is preceded by confession of wrongs and apologies where an individual or a leader of the group apologizes to other group leader as a sign of reconciliation. If the aggrieved accepts the apology, and believes the offender's remorse, he stands up, looks around and gives a lengthy speech which he concludes by saying *"Ca yë pälikä,"* meaning the offending group has been forgiven. In case it is an individual, the term, *ca ji pälikä"* meaning, you are forgiven is used instead. The conditions of forgiveness involve justice, repentance, admission of guilt, and a commitment to make peace going forward. *Pälikä* to the Nuer is a theme that must always be incorporated in peace building. It includes formal moral acts, changes in behaviour as an evidence of profound human transformation. Individual person among the Nuer people seeks to find harmony between him or her and the world around. In order to do this, every behaviour pattern is conceived in terms of kinship relations. Nuer individual believes that the Supreme Being *Kuoth nhial* or *Tutg*äär in creating a human being, endowed him/her with a conscience and an awareness of the moral expectation that is concretely reflected in moral issues. Thus, individual is expected to respond appropriately to the creator's demands and to comply with the requirements of the ancestors and societal agents.

A Nuer individual is expected to behave in a specific way, fulfill expected social roles, and conform to societal values. Any disregard of these demands comes with spiritual ramifications. They must make every effort to avoid offending to the spiritual world. Kinship provides ideological identity and security. Each individual is expected to perform Nuer customs and perform certain moral obligations within a kinship. It is, therefore, the responsibility of everyone to observe the various moral values to avoid disturbing the relationship between the members of the community and the Supreme Being (*Kuoth Nhial)*.

CHAPTER SIX:
RELIGION

One God, many manifestations

It is generally accepted in Nilotic culture that there are many religious systems in South Sudan and it is therefore, impossible to talk of one type of religion as being uniquely Nilotes. There is diversity in religious concepts and practices in South Sudan which are expressed in different cultures and in African contexts. Although, the religious expressions are multiple, the philosophy underlying religious life is singular and one would argue that the religions of Africa are similar enough to talk of African Traditional Religion (ATR) in a generic sense. They share a sufficient number of characteristics which seems to be a coherent philosophy underlying different expressions of their religions. The expressions of thought vary considerably in their application of basic beliefs. In South Sudan, African Indigenous Religion (AIR) has a long oral history which was passed on over from one generation to another by word of mouth until recent attempts at documentation.

The reference "African Indigenous Religion" presents an assumed unitary portrait of the religions of the Nilotic people as it is with other regions in African societies. Though it is true that many features of religion and their practice are similar across African continent, it would be erroneous to assume that all African religion(s) are the same. Hence, it has been suggested that the right label for the religions of African people reflect the religious plurality within the continent's religious landscape. The above description of the religion of AIR, is an emphasis being placed on the traditional aspect of the religion as opposed to other world's religions such as Christian and Islam, which, due to the process of contextualization, are now interpreted as African religions.

This description is also in line with the views of Pritchard (1956), who opined that the inference that can be drawn is that these different spirits are not thought of as independent gods but in some ways as hypostases of the modes and attributes of a single God (Pritchard, 1956). In all the analysis and descriptions given, this text has taken the position that the Nuer have no proper name for God. They simply call god *kuoth*, spirit and if they wish to distinguish the deity in speech, they can only do so by a qualifying clause. Therefore, with this understanding, the Nuer may not easily distinguish in the mind from the God of a neighbouring ethnic communities and the titles by which other people call the creator do not present to them any challenge or contradiction which might lead to more precise metaphysical definition. Since Nuer word for God is *kuoth* it simply means that any other spiritual being is also *kuoth*. This in itself, apart from the absence of any organized cult and developed political institutions, has allowed easy entrance to foreign spirits (Pritchard, 1956).

The Nuer speak of ''*kuth piny*'', spirits of the below or of the earth, in contrast with the ''*kuth nhial*'' spirits above. The Nuer put their argument on the fact that all spirits of the below are believed to have fallen from above, and inevitably so because the above is the house of big god –spirit from which other small spirits (gods) descend from. The Nuer think about them that they are conceived of as being still in the above, though they are also conceived of as immanent in creatures and things on earth and they are then opposed in thought to the spirits of the above. It can be argued that the Nuer regards these spirits as beings of the same importance as *kwoth nhial*, whom they manifest differently.

Manifestations (*Ngäth*)
This section further examines the manifestations, relevance and application of the Nuer traditional religious practices, partly before Arab migration into Sudan in 18th century and the arrival of European missionaries in the 19th century. These self-identities are shaped through acceptance of adaptation to these foreign religions that spread throughout South Sudan to the present day and have contributed to the religious challenges facing the Nuer cultural traditions.

 Generally, different religions present rich variety of facts worldwide. The ritual acts and doctrinal tenants within each religion do indeed exhibit a certain similarity; they bear the stamp of that particular religion, but they differ in characters from one another. The corresponding data in different religions are very numerous and entirely unique phenomena hardly ever occur. For examples, sacrifices take place almost in all religions, although in different forms. The concept of "prayers" is common to its various forms. For instance, "ritual purification" is a practice that occurs in most religions bearing religious significance (Kristensen, 1968). Although the text does not intend to compare religions as units, but there is need to highlight Nuer religious values that they have had for several decades as their cultural beliefs. In the process, given the interaction with other Nilotic religions, having similar facts and phenomena that bring them together, an element of comparison is unavoidable.

African Traditional Religion (ATR) is a complex phenomenon that is basically connected with Nuer culture and in which it finds its expressions as explained by some scholars (Lugira, 1999, Gehman, 1989 and Byaruhuanga-Akiiki, A.B.T) who define ATR from a perspective of life. They all agree that religion in Africa means life, the reality that is lived in a cobweb of relationship. The major actors or actresses involved in those relationships include the master creator, human beings, living and dead, all plants, animals, birds, molecules, atoms, particles and whatever the creator created that is visible and invisible. The best term to describe "God" in ATR is "the Supreme Being", who is understood not only as source of morality but also its guardian and custodian. The Supreme Being is mainly concerned in the code of conduct of His people and supports and rewards those who do good and punishes those who fail to abide by the laid down moral standards (Getui, 2008).

African Traditional Religion is constituted of five parts: beliefs, practices, ceremonies and festivals, religious objects and places, values and morals and religious officials and leaders (Mbiti 1975). Thus, in ATR, God, is perceived as Supreme Being, creator, and sustainer of his creation; provider, and the one who rules over the universe. Within ATR and its worldview, man is the center of the universe whose main responsibilities is to maintain harmony between the visible (material) world and the invisible one (god, ancestors and other spirits). Fulfilling that responsibility is a sign of moral character and ensures the harmony between all elements of the universe.

According to oral history, African philosophy is basically anthropocentric, where man is at the center of existence and African peoples see everything in its relation to this central position of man. In this sense, God is the explanation of man's origin and sustenance. God is perceived as being active in human history. Thus, for Africans, God is in theory transcendent, but in practice immanent and that the position God takes in African religion is not necessarily that of redeemer. As there is no condition from which humanity is in need of deliverance, African Traditional Religion sees worshipping God as imploring the provider to keep on doing so. God is not worshipped in order to gain salvation.

Some Nilotic traditional believers in South Sudan explain that adherents of the indigenous religions are very conservative; such like Nuer religion resisted the influence of modernism prefigured by the colonial era, including the introduction of Islam, Christianity, Western education and improved medical facilities. The Nuer cherish their traditions; they worship god (*kuoth*) with sincerity because their worship is meaningful to them and hold tenaciously to their covenant that binds them together. Their religion is based mainly on oral transmission and though not documented, but richly manifested in people's hearts, minds, rituals and religious functions. Indigenous religion has no founders or reformers like Gautama the Buddha, Asoka, Christ, or Muhammad. It is not the religion of one hero and has no desire to propagate the religion, or to evangelize. However, the adherents are loyal worshippers of their god (Awolalu, 1976) whom they manifest in different ways.

Nuer culture offers an inclusive understanding of the "people". The Nuer language has two religious words for "people": *cuk*, (singular *cok)* means "peoples" in the inclusive sense in contrast to the word *naath* that denotes "people" in the particular sense of the Nuer themselves. The latter term is used by the Nuer to identify themselves separately from others and to infer sense of ethnic distinction. The Nuer phrase *kɔndial labnɛ gaatkuoth* ("we are all God's children"), explains that the Nuer see other people the same way they believe God sees the whole humanity in their diverse cultures without distinction. The Nuer uses this phrase to show their relationship with the almighty God, which they called (*Kuoth, Tutgäär or Kuoth Nhial)*, meaning super being that makes an important point in the Nuer worldview.

Nuer people believe that ancestors act as mediators between god and humans. In mediating to the supernatural, the Nuer manifestation is bound upon the concept of existent of God everywhere *Kuoth jom (*god in the air). The Prophets and spiritual beings are driving their powers from God in the air through expression of spreading ash, grass leave; leave of the plant, Tabaco leave and sprinkling of water in the air. Such expressions convinced the individual and group that they are in spiritual relation with God. They also believe that the spirit of person strike by lightening *(cholwic)* exists in spirit and people turn to for guidance in time of danger. Nuer believe that this person still exists in spirit symbolized by offering of sacrifices often and supplication for peace and protection in time of danger. Nuer believe a person taken by *(Cholwic)* or literally strike by lightening can appear at sunrise or at dawn when scarifies are offered (*Päät*) as process of mediating with spirit. This believe of *cholwic* is shared throughout Nuer society and illuminates this aspect very clearly when they present knowledge of African people of the transcendental world as a pool of power. The Supreme Being (*Tutgäär*) would then be the culmination of this pool of power and not necessarily a person. In other words, *Tutgäär* is seen as the peak of the spiritual hierarchy. The spirits of the deceased ancestors reside in this deistic and dynamistic spiritual realm. Nuer Religion exhibits a specific social understanding of the place of the individual in community. There is a dynamic natural bond between the individual, the extended family, the clan or the society as a whole and the ancestors, nature and God. Nuer religion binds and does not divide a community. The group shares similar sacred beliefs and practices; their religion determines every aspect of community life. The group becomes a sacred community. The sanctity of the community is maintained by regulations pertaining to proper behaviour. Such behaviour is governed by moral sanctity and ethical norms prohibiting individual or group to infringe to societal taboos. Getui noted that taboos are sacred prohibitions placed upon some people or some things, which makes them untouchable or unmentionable. Indeed, taboos are dos and don't dos or social restrictions result from long traditions of a community. The Nuer perceive taboos as both social, and religious in that it has to do with what the *kuoth nhial* (God in the sky) forbids. The purpose of taboos in Nuer community is to promote the needed sense mutual responsibility and solidarity. Taboos therefore serve to help people maintain good morals. To break taboos, therefore, may bring disorder not only to the individual but the entire community. Taboos therefore inculcate spiritual and moral values to individuals and to the community in general and must abide by honesty and respect of *kuoth nhial* (God in the sky or above). Improper or unjust behaviour toward fellow members of the community disrupts harmony and damages the sanctity of the community. Only through ritual reparation can sanctity and harmony be restored. That is to the advantage of the group supersedes individual wishes.

The Nuer concept of Prophets (*göök*) is both particular and universal, because the Nuer accepts that all these Prophets are genuine messengers from God. Prophets may receive revelations in a variety of ways including dreams, prophecy, symbols and events. However, the revelations received, are considered to be authentic and valid for the particular people among from whom a Prophet comes. Nuer Prophets are generally regarded as the custodians of morality among the communities who believe in them. Prophets play very important roles of intermediaries and monitors of human behaviour on behalf of God (*kuoth*). They act as guardians of public morality and command the good behaviour of human beings and likewise punish those who break the rules as laid down by the Supreme Being.

The Nuer believe that God is the Creator (*Cääk*) of all that exists. *Cääk* is also the word that the Nuer language uses for "creation". The fact that Creator and creation are denoted by the same word is of great significance in Nuer belief. Creation does not spring form nothing, but is understood to come from God, as an extension of God's own reality. This means that creation itself is infused by God's being, and this is expressed through the Nuer belief in a spiritual cosmology, creation being full of spirits that are understood as being part of *kuoth nhial*. The Nuer understanding of *kuoth* includes the whole range of spiritual beings: ancestral spirits, household spirits, talking spirits, sky spirits, and earth spirits.

It is through these spiritual intermediaries that are inseparable form *kuoth* himself that creation is sustained, and it is to these intermediaries, therefore, the Nuer turn to when they address *Kuoth* in worship. There is also water spirit as part of mediation and understanding of God. This believes and practice is found among the western Nuer community of *Dok* from *Duog* sub-clan. *Duog* has water spirit refers as *Moth*. The community believed that *moth* could mediate to god through water spirit and is consulted when such need arises. They offer sacrifices at the riverside to ensure safe passage of people or their livestock when crossing the Nile even if savaged crocodile infested does not pose threat when *moth* is consulted said one community member – Kuong Ter. They believe that god is found everywhere, in every culture, and meets individuals in his own ways and has power which extends to all peoples (*cuk*). God protects all people, and god embraces every human being in justice and equality. To express the individual quality of human experience of god, the Nuer language uses the Word *Ran* meaning "person as distinct from "people". As god relates equally to all "peoples" *(cuk),* every person (*ran*) has a direct relationship with god.

The Nuer believe that there is only one God with many names in different cultures and societies. Their concept, 'One god, many names' justifies that different people can perceive god in different ways but that would not bring conflict to hinder co-existence of the communities as long each person respect other traditional beliefs. This perception of god within Nilotic people in South Sudan in general and the Nuer people in particular, is that god is professed differently by different communities. For example, believing in god in different ways does not create problems to the Nuer when they come in contact with other people's ways of approaching god. The Nuer (*Naath*) are always proud of themselves and show no interest of other's people's ways of life, but are aware that in religious matters, neighbouring people differ. Some know about Dinka religious beliefs and ceremonies. A few are aware about Islam which they perceive as religion of Arab traders and that they have their own form of worshiping God. They also respect those who believe in Christianity. The text does not compare the religions with one another as units, but highlights Nuer religious values that had for several decades existed as their cultural beliefs and considered absolute as they interact with other religions having similar facts and phenomena that bring them together.

Relevance of Nuer religion (*Luöt ngäthä kuoth kä naath*)
This section describes the relevance of Nuer religion in conjunction with other African traditional believers. I have noted most of the times, Nilotic, particularly Nuer Christians seek comfort in their own religious symbol systems, even though these may not correspond exactly to those inculcated and expected by their Christian leaders. As Magesa also observed, indeed, these are often symbols and rituals that church leaders have explicitly condemned. (Magesa, 1974). This description shows that the African Christian rejects remarkably little of their former non-Christian outlook. In other words, she does not recant a religious philosophy in him or her. Consequently, the African Christian operates with two thought-systems (Shorter, 1975). Shorter, further pointed out that the relevance and influence of African Religion in Post-Apartheid South Africa and beyond at once, and both of them are close to each other. Each is only superficially modified by the other. Okwuosa has pointed out to the writing in 1960 by the Nigerian, Chief Obafemi Awolowo, who made substantially the same point with reference to

his own country (Okwuosa, 1977). He asserts that Christian and Muslim beliefs and practices are, with many Nigerians, nothing but appearances and social cover-ups: at heart and in the privacy of their lives, most Nigerian Christians and Moslems are African religious traditionalists.

Actually, Nuer contextual theology embraces other religious faiths in some of their traditional practices. For example, the Nuer may perform traditional, Christian and even Islamic marriages according to their customs. Nuer contextual theology live side by side with their high levels of respect to Christianity and Islam and many still retain their beliefs and rituals that are characteristic of traditional religions. Meaning the Nuer are traditionalist, despite their religious affiliations. In similar manner, Nuer traditional religion has its solidest element in traditional contextual and exerts possibly the greatest influence upon the thinking and living of the Nuer people. The importance of Nuer theology cannot be down played, for Nuer who are converted to other faiths such as Christianity or Islam; still retain their dominant motivation for their religious life in Nuer traditions. Nuer people 'come out of African religion, nonetheless, they don't take off their old-style religiosity despite the changes taking place nowadays. Of course, Nuer religion has and still undergoing many changes, due to the influence of Christianity and Islam which are generally on the surface, heart-rending the material side of life and only beginning to reach the deeper levels of thinking pattern, language content, the relevance and influence of traditional religion in post-Apartheid mental images, emotions, beliefs and response in situations of need are cases to note. For the Nuer of South Sudan, the influence of Christianity and Islam and their impacts and memories of agonies cannot easily go away in the minds of people. Yet, African traditional concepts still form the essential background of many African peoples. Meaning, their innermost religious determination remains overwhelmingly African theology. For example, in South Sudan, many converts publicly claim the new intended meaning while unconsciously ascribing to them a different one that is traditional beliefs. They come as people whose world-view is shaped according to African contextual theologies from which the Nuer religion is build.

The Nuer religion is an agent of social reconstruction which provides people with a view of the world and inspires new ideas. This social change of the society keeps renewing itself to deal with the changing traditional beliefs. Many Nuer people still express high levels of belief in the protective power of sacrificial offerings and sacred objects. The Nuer believe in the evil eye, or the ability of certain people to cast malevolent curses or spells in most countries in African continent. Mbiti gives examples from five countries (Tanzania, Cameroon, Democratic Republic of Congo, Senegal and Mali) where majority of people express this belief (Mbiti, 1975). Comparatively, like Berger and Luckmann, Mugambi are convinced that African traditional religion has an important role in the social reconstruction of a society as that of the Nuer. As both object and agent of social reconstruction, Nuer religion provides the world view which synthesizes everything cherished by the individuals as corporate members of the community. It is my personal opinion that Nuer religion is the most vital project for the people who are undergoing a rapid change as in post-colonial Africa. In Jaspers (1972), Mugambi is greatly influenced by Karl Jaspers' positive appraisal of mythical thinking; according to him the myth tells a story and expresses intuitive insights, rather than universal concepts. This prompts him to argue that a society, which is incapable of making its own myths or re-interpreting its old ones, becomes extinct. Agree with this statement and in my view, the vision of theology of reconstruction in Nuer contextual theology, is a vital project of re-mythologization, in which the African theologians should be engaged, discerns new symbols and new metaphors in which to recast the central message of the Gospel in line with the Nuer culture who still adhered to their traditions.

Application of Nuer Religion (*Läth lät Kuoth kä Naath*)

The application of Nuer religion is significant in the Nuer society and should not be downplayed. As Paul F. Knitter, notes, nothing comes before people's religious identity and convictions (Paul F. Knitter, 2005, SMT, Vol. 93, No.). If this identity is threatened, everything must be sacrificed or ventured in order to preserve it. Additionally, a study of African Traditional Religion is tantamount to a religious dialogue. If it is done, for instance by Christian theologians, it amounts to a dialogue between Christianity and African Traditional Religion. Moreover, there will be no peace among nations without better dialogue among religions. I agree with this opening statement of this great Theologian Paul F Knitter, and in my opinion, the need for a more intensive philosophical and theological dialogue among religions takes religious plurality seriously in theological terms, accepts the challenge of the other religions and investigates their significance for each person's own religion. It is important to note that this engagement is crucial considering that the dialogue between, for instance, African Traditional Religion and other religions such as Christianity and Islam has never been a real conversation in South Sudan.

In South Sudan for example, the contact between Christianity, Islam and African Traditional Religion has historically been predominantly a monologue, bedeviled by assumptions prejudicial against the latter, with Christianity and Islam culturally more vocal and ideologically more aggressive. Therefore, what Nuer people have heard until now is largely Christianity and Islam speaking about African Traditional Religion, not African Religion speaking for itself. Thus, there is need to study African Religion as a way of making it enter into a form of dialogue with other religions as it is by this that African traditional believers (ATB) will experience genuine shalom that will bring wholeness in Africa. All religious leaders including African Traditional Believers have a duty to usher in a new dawn in Africa today.

The application of Nuer religion is in different ways: the roles of the Prophets were very important to make clear to the people what *ŋuɔt* (literally "to cut"), or vow covenant, requires of them of their moral lives. As well as covenant, *ŋuɔt* means rules and regulations (laws) that the Nuer apply across all aspects of their lives, as communities and individual. These includes; rules that are agreed and applied by the Nuer to punish those who have committed crimes and broken the covenant, and rituals by which those who have committed evil can restore themselves to covenantal relationship with God and their communities. In this respect, *ŋuɔt* regulate sacrifices that are to be made to God (*kuoth*) as means of moral and spiritual restitution.

Ŋuɔt are especially important in Nuer religious terms and apply in conflict resolution and reconciliation, providing an agreed body of rituals that bind people together in their relationship with God. This is quite evident in the importance of the late 19ᵗʰ century Prophet ŋundɛŋ Bong who stands in the Nuer tradition as the great Prophet of peace and reconciliation. For more details see (Riam, 2022 and Johnson, 1978), when ŋundeŋ instituted principles of compensation that were intended to reduce conflicts and created harmony among the people. These principles have had universal effect, ensuring the well-being not just of the Nuer people but also of all the neighbouring people.

One other important element in connection with application of the Nuer religious beliefs that have bearing on the covenant is the oath (*yai*), which is also sworn before the *Kuär Muon* (Leopard Skin Chief). There are two forms of oath in the Nuer traditional system: *kueŋ/kuil* or *käp tang* ("to hold the spear-shaft") which is used in a variety of circumstances, while *mäth* ('to drink") is the form often employed in cases of homicide. The taking of an oath is collective process by the accused party. In the former ceremony both the accuser and accused are expected to take part. In the latter, were there is no known accused, those suspected and all their kinsmen are required to participate and shoulder the responsibility. Another important aspect is the casting of lots in case of denial of offends, the subjects are asked by the spiritual leader known as (*KuärTuac*) after performing invocation of mediating supernatural to reveal the culprit responsible for the misconduct. In such case bad omen is believed to befall the offender or in some instant, the person can voluntarily confess. In addition to Nuer rules of *Ŋuɔt kueng* is being considered as an important element of enforcing traditional system of oath, where a hole is dug and the suspects are asked to jump over the hole. This can reveal the offenders or through confession bringing about forgiveness and reconciliation through communion and fellowship with one another, giving way to the spiritual leaders and chiefs without loss of dignity and oaths as they observed Nuer moral values.

Nuer attitude towards other people
Establishing the foregoing narrative of Nuer relations has necessarily entailed consideration of the history of Nuer contact with the outside world. These brief events of Nuer contact are usefully shortened here and provides basis for assessing the role of external factors in Nuer attitude towards outsiders. This subsection highlights two different perceptions towards other nationalities: Nuer attitude towards the outside world, such as colonial invaders, second their attitudes towards others faiths.

The Nuer international relations with the outside world have been problematic. This was because authorities and powers, which came to Nuer land like British, Turkish and Egyptian governments, only came in contact with the Nuer through Nuer local rivals. Some Nuer elders with fresh memories, told me that the Dinka people deliberately misinformed the aforesaid authorities and powers about Nuer people in almost all aspects. This evolved into misconception of the Nuer by the aforementioned authorities and powers and their allies with vested interests in Nuerland. This proved willful since the colonial governments only hired interpreters from Dinka communities, who were Nuer rivals and cruelly and mistakenly reported wrong things about the Nuer. For example, one Dinka interpreter reporting to foreign authority, stated that the White Nile Dinka withdrew northward from the Sobat under the pressure of constant Nuer attacks about thirty years earlier (Kelly, 1985). That made it harder for the Nuer to reach out to interact directly with those foreigners who want to deal with them.

This Nuer attitude towards outsiders is also linked to the language used by the missionary's personnel who first came to Southern Sudan for evangelisation. The missionaries came with a ready terminology to Nuerland during their proselytisation for the people they envisioned to convert. As Johnson (2015) clarifies; the missionaries brought with them the word "pagan" from the days when they were battling for souls with the old temple religions of the Roman Empire. They found pagan galore in the Southern Sudan when they first arrived in the 19th century. Nonetheless the term "pagan" is suggestive of Christian's propaganda and in the 1950s and 1960s as the Sudan and other African countries became independent, missionaries became increasingly uncomfortable with using such a hurtful term. He also pointed out that there was a strong dialogue between missionaries and anthropological studies of African religions in this connection and while British Social Anthropologists in Sudan and East Africa had rejected the term "animist", which appeared to have more neutral and scientific value than paganism (Johnson, 2015). This was how the Nuer started to perceive missionaries as foreigners who had come to destroy their cultural identity and religious values not because the Nuer do not know God as the missionaries thought. The Nuer know God and that could be one of the reasons why a dialogue was initiated between missionaries and Anthropologists discussed above in connection with the terms "animist" "pagan" which the former appeared to have more neutral and scientific value than paganism. It is important to note that it was at this time the British forces were combating the Nuer Prophets, such as Guɛk Ngundɛŋ and Dual Diu. Thus, Nuer attitude towards missionaries' personnel was no any different from the colonisers fighting them. The Nuer then, remained a cold and dangerous human predicament, caused by outsiders one elder said. This appears to show the ugly face preconception and bias to the Nuer who always value rights of others and share common good with them. This is true as we can see from Nuer perspective-attitude towards other faiths who came in contact with them directly as observed by Evans-Pritchard.

Nuer attitude towards other faiths
Evans-Pritchard observation about Nuer attitudes to others is correct as my observations and understanding are concern. He explained that; when a Nuer comes into contact with different people who speak of their own religious beliefs and practices, he shows that he does not regard them as having a different God from his own but merely as having different names and a different manner of communicating with God. For example, a *Dinka* prays God in heaven, which he calls (*nhialic*). Similarly, the Muslims and Christian pray to God under different other names. Although the Nuer have borrowed from their neighbours the lesser spirit (gods) like that of the *Dinka* called "deng" and the *Shilluk* spirit called, "*nyikang*", all of which are expressed in the songs of the Nuer Prophet Ngundɛŋ Bong described earlier in our historical chapter one above. The Nuer have not taken their deities such as *Nhialic* (God) in *Dinka* and *Juok* (God) in *Shilluk*. The Nuer believe that *Juok* and *nhialic* are one God have different titles among different peoples (Pritchard, 1956). By traditions, the Nuer religion expresses the relationship between God and the people through the concept of covenant that denotes an

inviolable bond both between the creator and all the creation and between all peoples. The Nuer Prophets are mainly concerned with the welfare of the Nuer and other ethnic communities. This perception clearly indicates the markedly monolithic tendency of Nuer religious thoughts, which I presume binds all Nilotic traditional believers together with their God.

With this Nuer attitude towards other religious traditions, it can therefore, be argued that when the missionaries came to South Sudan for evangelization, it did not create the Nuer people a problem to hear them preaching God's word, because the Nuer believe that there is only one God; that already exist under different titles and different names from their own. This is evident from the way Nuer regard the beliefs of other religious traditions; though Islam had made no impression on them, but aware that Arab traders have their own form of worshiping their God which they call *"Allah"*. Christian missionaries on the other hand had made some progress, but negligible due to cultural barrier. This can be seen in Pritchard's work after conclusion of his research in 1956: there were only 464 Nuer coverts (250 Catholics and 214 Protestants). He named those missions as American Presbyterian at Nasser (Nasir) on the Sobat (founded in 1913), Catholic at *Yoah nyang* on the Bahr el Ghazal (founded in 1929), and Anglican at *Leer* to the west of the Nile (founded in 1932) and *Juaibor* to the east of the Nile (founded in 1936) (Pritchard, 1956). Those missions later on encountered with the Nuer and through their evangelizations started to condemn indigenous religious practices without proper understanding the relevance of the Nuer moral values.

The strength of Nuer moral values lay on interpersonal relationship and on the human relationship with their creator (*Cääk*). The moral crisis in Nuer society today can be attributed largely social tie break down, self-interest and lack of knowledge of their culture at the expense of the common good. The moral issues today have been stripped of the divine connotations and mainly for this reason that no one takes moral values seriously. As a result, Nuer culture is confronted with morally decadent society in which the solution to these problems is to place Nuer moral values on a strong foundation within the culture transformation processes and would require Nuer people themselves to seriously revive their traditions in order to preserve moral values now being threaten by many factors including; wars and modernization trends.

Arabisation and Islamisation Policies
It was not until the 13th century that the Christian kingdoms went into decline, the *Baqt* treaty was broken by increasing pressures from Arab Muslim traders who settled in Nubia, and the conquest of Makuria by the Mamluk Egyptian army in 1276 marked the inaugurated of the Muslim rule. In the 16th century the Islamic Funj Sultanate replaced the last Christian kingdom of Alwa (Holt and Daly, 2000). In the early 19th century the territory of the Funj Sultanate fell under the political rule of the Ottoman Turkish rulers of Egypt period (1821-1881). At that time many Nubians were killed, some enslaved and the survival those fled to the Upper Nile South Sudan where they mounted a determined resistance to the southward expansion of Islamic power. This period saw a vast extension of the enslavement and Islamisation of Black Africans as a means of maintaining a huge slave army to police the expanding Turco-Egyptian territories.

By 1856 Arab Muslim traders were already in Bahr el Ghazal, where they built relationships with the local chiefs to facilitate the movements of goods. During the first half of 19th century, the slave trade became an essential part of the Turco-Egyptian and Northern Sudanese economy, supplying Egypt's domestic and military needs. Meanwhile, some northern Sudanese cadres were being educated at the Azhar Mosque-University in Cairo. Sudanese Islam continued to be deeply influenced by Sufism, as it had been during the centuries of the Funj Sultanate. While the *Qairiya* Order was traditionally the most powerful *Sufi* movement in Northern Sudan, as elsewhere in Sub-Saharan Africa, the 19th Century saw the rise of new Sufi orders that emphasized more indigenous forms of *Sufism*. In Sudan it was the *Khatmiyya* Order that dominated the religious scene, and made a point of maintaining good political terms with the Turco-Egyptian administration. But growing resentment against the Turco-Egyptian colonial presence and its policies especially of taxation, led many Muslims to yearn for a more dynamic religious leadership that would defend local interests more effectively than did the *Khatmiyya* Order. From 1881-1898 was the Mhadi State. The coming of *Mahdiyya* never succeeded in extending its power permanently into the equatorial regions of the Upper Nile region. Karam Allah, one of the *Ansâr*, managed to take Amadi town on Yei River in Equatoria, but only with considerable difficulty and for a short period. After the *Mahdî's* death in 1885, his successors withdrew from the region where they made little religious impact (Holt and Daly, 2000). The Anglo-Egyptian administration of Sudan took over following the defeat of the *Mahdist* state untill 1946 when the colonial administration decided that Sudan was ready for independence as a united country. During its four decades, Sudan was administered in two regions, the North and the South. The missionaries working side by side with colonial governments were interested in development in the South that led to its Christianization, while the North consolidated its unity under Islam and Arabisation policies. Those division compounded historic distinctions between Muslim North and an increasing Christian South and historic distinctions between Arabs and Africans, and added to the tensions between the South and the North that were to continue a divisive factor in Sudanese political and religious life thereafter.

Throughout the history of Sudan as independence state, Islamisation and Arabisation policies were perused vigorously. Abboud government in 1964 took drastic measures soon it was in power. Sunday was replaced by Friday as the religious holiday in the South, conforming to the Muslim practice of the North. This had immense symbolic meaning for the Southerners who perceived this as an attempt to coerce them to accept Islamic and Arab culture. Secondly, Christians were not allowed to pray anywhere except on Sundays, and only in Churches. Muslims on the other hand enjoyed freedom of worship which they practiced anywhere. Southerners were induced to embrace Islam. For example, an exceptional example was Chief Jambo of the Moru tribe who changed his name to Ibrahim when he was persuaded to accept Islam (Riam, 2022). On economic spheres, Article 16 of the 1973 constitution, stipulated that the Democratic Republic of Sudan "shall be guided by Islam being the religion of the majority of its people and the state shall express its values" (Sudan Government, 1973).

In the context of implementing Islamic principles, the network of Islamic banks enlisted Islamic cadres and experts in economic institutions. National Islamic Front (NIF) became a major player in economic sector. The Northern banking system was Islamized through the introduction of interest-free Islamic banking practices, independent of the Bank of Sudan. The Faisal Islamic Bank of Sudan, followed by Islamic Co-operative Development Bank Tadamum Islamic Bank of Western Sudan, and the Bank of Northern Sudan. Just only to mention a few.

Christianity in Southern Sudan
The introduction of Christianity to South Sudan by European missionaries, all doctrines, traditions and customs of the Church have been disseminated to the indigenous people throughout the medium of foreign culture. The western missionaries in general followed a policy that labelled whatever cultural ethos did not harmonize with the European way of thinking and lifestyle as unchristian. Their attitude has persisted from the beginning of the missionary era up to the present day in the life of the Church as an institution. This is reflected in the liturgy, catechetic, doctrine and canonical norms of the church in South Sudan.

Since then, the Church has remained western on South Sudanese soil on the plea that all European is Christian and all indigenous cultures could intrinsically hardly qualify as Christian. During that missionary era, most missionaries persuaded the Nuer converts to abandon and denounce their heritage and imitate missionaries' lifestyles. The Nuer converts were then expected to be divorced from their own culture in order to embrace the gospel. This was impossible hence the missionaries' approach was perceived as external policy designed to destroy Nuer self rule, because of the negative attitude of missionaries towards their cultural and religious heritage that remained unresolved.

The unresolved tensions between the Nuer indigenous culture and the Christian beliefs and messages on this kind of marriage are already manifesting themselves in major churches and particularly in the Presbyterian Church of South Sudan. A good example is what happened on June 13, the day after Archbishop Daniel Deng consecrated Bishop Ruben Akurdit Ngong. Followers of his defeated rival in the May 14 election announced they were quitting the Episcopal Church to form the Lutheran Church of Sudan quoting lack of spiritual and physical development in the diocese alongside the diocese's toleration of ghost marriages, saying the Nuer tribal custom was incompatible with Christian message.

It is noted that since the advent of Christianity in Nuer Nation, polygamy has been portrayed in church spheres as problematic and in many instances it has been condemned and despised. Some Nuer polygamous families grieved when after conversion they were encouraged to divorce and neglect a part of their families. Many have been denied Christian sacraments such as baptism and the Eucharist if they failed to comply with the demand of the church. Sometimes the church sanctioned the banishment of some of family members, while in the same breath the church preached the indissolubility of marriage.

Let me briefly highlight the first World Missionary Conference Meeting held at Edinburgh in 1910 attended only by the western Missionaries that considered the question of polygamy as many participants were convinced that polygamy was not only forbidden in the New Testament by the divine injunction, but that it was part of the fallen nature of the human race (Getui, 2008). The participants further argued that polygamy was one of the gross evils in the heathen society which must at all costs be ended. In some instances, some of churches like the Presbyterian Church of South Sudan grudgingly accepted the first wife as having been married while other subsequent wives were deemed to be living in adulterous relationships. This means that monogamy was made a condition for marriage. Hence, polygamous families could not be fully accepted in church membership. Women in a polygamous marriage except the first wife were not allowed to be baptized or take part in the holy sacrament as it was considered sinful to be in a polygamous marriage. The husband was considered the main culprit and therefore was not allowed to be baptized or take part in the Holy Communion under any circumstance and was not considered to be a member of any Church.

Similarly, the Anglican Lambeth Conference of 1888 allowed local bishops to decide under what circumstance the wives of polygamous husbands could be admitted to church membership as Christians upheld monogamy, believing that it was the highest and purest form of marriage in accordance with biblical command even as they felt that this was the only form of marriage that God accepted as three or four persons cannot become one. Their arguments were based on the teaching of Paul in the New Testament who states that anyone who aspired to become a church official must be a husband of one wife and married only once (1Corinthians 7). This was interpreted to mean that every Christian was commanded to have one wife and that this was God's will.

Let me explain some of the difficulties the Nuer converts have faced in recent past, in South Sudan: The Catholic Church which has been advocating for monogamous marriages, where only unmarried youth, the first wives in the family and children are baptized. For example, in 1998, only about 30 couples in Old Fangak County - Jonglei State in South Sudan - were married in the Church, including 30,000 people. As a result, there are three main groups that were officially allowed to participate in communion: Children and youth before they marry; missionaries and religious leaders; widows and old people who are considered not to be intimate with their spouse (Schmidt, 2015). The Nuer catechists in this situation were expected by the diocese to marry in the church so that they can live monogamously in the hope that they would opt for the sacrament later on. While serving the people, they would have time to reflect on this issue and sort it out with their families. The pastoral experience has shown that it was wise to let a man have several children and live some years in a stable traditional marriage before entering the sacramental bond with his wife. Many catechists in Nuer churches taught catechism and led liturgical prayers in the absence of the priest while at the same time they were excluded from receiving the Eucharist because establishment of the church deemed them unclean. They were good enough to unite and nurture the Catholics in the Chapels but were considered so sinful that they would commit a sacrilege if they would commune at the altar of the Lord. The Bishops certainly would have preferred to allow only sacramentally married men to serve as catechists, but then, Catholic Chapels would be left abandoned. In order to secure a Catholic presence in the countryside, they opted for the lesser malevolent.

My interaction with the former Moderator of the Presbyterian Church of South Sudan Rev.Deng (2012) held the same view as that of the Catholic Church. He told me that Polygamy is a road block to baptism or for those already baptized to take Holy Communion. He argues that the enforcement of this policy has created painful stress in South Sudan Christian homes, mostly in Upper Nile region (Deng, 2012). For example, while evangelizing to the Anyuak community around Pochalla County, Rev. Harvey Hoekstra (Missionary) was confronted with the question of polygamy. The Anyuak King who was a new convert, wanted to be baptized, but he had four (4) wives, a scenario that led to him being denied access to the Presbyterian Church membership. The argument was based on the fact that monogamy is understood as a general rule by Christians. Polygamy is currently rejected by most Christian denominations in South Sudan. The predominant Christian position is that polygamy is morally wrong, and a number of passages in the New Testament have been cited as discouraging polygamy.

However, from many community leaders, provided different views to that of the church. They suggest that although a good number of South Sudanese people have converted to Christianity, polygamy still is the cultural ideal of most Nuer men. But, due to economic and productive factors, many men contract only a single marriage in recent times, yet, a significant proportion of domestic unions involve the marriage of one man to a number of wives. In some wealthy families, men have from 20 to 50 wives. These marriage customs tend to create a final link across wide political and geographic spaces. We have already noted in the proceeding chapters that Nuer marriage is legally defined through the exchange of bride-wealth in the form of cattle. Among the Nuer, co-wives often share the responsibilities of preparing meals on a rotating basis, although a woman always attends to the needs of her own children first. Because they never learn to cook in their youth, the men are dependent upon women to prepare food for them throughout their lives.

 Truly, these are some of the real challenges that modern church is facing within the context of inculturation. Even though Christians may continue to insist that ideally monogamy is a more effective expression of human love and relationship, it does not give anyone a license to blindly condemn polygamy. The fact that the Church remains committed to their condemnation of polygamy does not in itself produce an ideal form of marriage that is functional in Nuer Society. However, the Bible does not condemn nor condone polygamy. One would argue that there is need to appreciate the practice of polygamy which is so deeply intertwined with Nuer culture that the Church has now found difficult to extricate itself from its social implications. It will be a great mistake in my view, to isolate the marriage of Christians from the question of marriage in the general body of the Nuer Community. We cannot redeem the individual's attitude to marriage without redeeming that of the Nuer society in which one belongs. It is to be recalled that culturally, polygamy acted as a security that the family will be continued and the prospect of a large family were imminent. The benefits of polygamy which were seen in the past are still relevant and are accepted and practiced by Nuer Christians. These benefits include helping to stabilize family life by ensuring that divorce was curtailed as one man was allowed to marry from different communities. In rural areas and particularly among the pastoralist communities like the Nuer, polygamy has become more of an asset than a liability as it increases the labour force and gives a boost to food security. Nevertheless, polygamy remains a great challenge to the Church in South Sudan.

Independent religious movements

Both Evans–Pritchard on Nuer religions (1951) and Godfery Lienhardt of Divinity and experience had similar views: The religion of the Dinka (1961) described how indigenous religions were practiced and believed. For example, Prophets Ngundɛŋ of the Nuer, and Aianhdit of Dinka whose followers existed till these days. Those scholars did not show in their investigations whether these indigenous religions would still operate after Christianity and Islam have taken roots in the contemporary South Sudan. This is the purpose of this text to highlight the significance of indigenous practices outline below.

Ngundɛŋ Church

A good number of people among the Nuer Nation are still followers of African Indegenous religion such as; Ngundɛng's church -Ngundɛng being one of Nuer major Prophets referred to earlier in this text, which has significantly made an impact in terms of indigenous church growth. Ngundɛŋ church has currently many followers in Nuer nation especially in central and eastern Nuer with their new bible written in Nuer language (*thok Naath*) called "*Joknyälä*", which has a similar designed as that of the Quran in cover and chapters. It consists of 248 chapters from which Ngun*dɛŋ*'s prophecies are observed and preached. In 2022, I interviewed four religious leaders from Ngundɛŋ Church in Juba who told me how the structure of their governing system and its hierarchy look like. The details of their operation lie outside this text.

The Dinka Prophet Arianhdit

There are also other adherents of Dinka traditional religions known as Prophet Arianhdit (Great Ariath) which is still being practice in Dinka land and has significance number of followers. The Prophet Arianhdit was a man whose personal name was Bol Yol a Dinka of the spear-master clan of Pariath and a lineage of that clan which was important in his community among the then stormy Abiem Dinka (Lienhardt, 1961). Bol Yol was possessed by the Divinity towards the end of 1914 – 18 war and gave the name of his divinity as Arianhdit. He was also regarded especially inspired by his clan –divinity called 'DENG PIOL' as especially active in him. His followers the Dinka to this day maintain that Prophet Arianhdit wanted peace both between communities and the government but was misunderstood when his fellow Dinka carried lies to the then colonial government, was captured and exiled. Many years afterwards, he was allowed to return home to (Dinkaland) and started to bring around him members of his followers although he was now old and the government was well rooted. Like Prophet Ngundɛŋ Bong, Prophet Arianhdit made some prophecies during his priesthood advocating that: soon the Dinka and the government would live side by side and will interact with community. Arianhdit also propercised that there would be disasters for those who would not live at peace with their neighbours. The former prophecy points to the political development which were under the Anglo-Egyptian administration and possibly the 1930s Ordinance that administered southern provinces. The latter of course, perhaps the current political developments including conflicts, wars and disasters happening in the republic of South Sudan as we see today which some of his followers say are the words of Prophet Arianhdit composed in form of songs. Arianhdit was a great "charismatic personality whose name was and still being held in the highest respect by many Dinka even today.

Even though, it is difficult to provide an exact number of the followers of indegenous religion in South Sudan, some people would estimate these followers as more numerous. It is therefore, imperative to argue that the moral perspectives of indegenous religion are essentially alive throughout the country. Nilotic traditional concepts of reality and destiny are deeply rooted in their spirit world. With this understanding therefore, it is clear that the activities and actions of the spirit beings govern all social and spiritual phenomena. The lack of statistic as evident of the followers of indigenous religion paves way for further research. It is to be recalled that traditional beliefs are also enshrined in the Transitional Constitution of Republic of South Sudan 2011.

However, these traditions continue to suffer from lack of acceptance and inadequate understanding of their central tenets and essence. The two monotheistic traditions, Islam and Christianity, to which most Nuer have converted over the years, have developed a hostile attitude to Nuer tradition; Islam relegates it to *al-Jahilliyya*, the era of barbarism, and Christianity views it as pure paganism. In my opinion, this is not true. Christian theologians and Muslim clerics should wear good lenses to see beyond their midday shadows to discover biblical and quranic texts that would make their followers understand the meaning of religious pluralism that allows each religion apply its doctrine to its followers.

Indigenous Education

Education is an expansive term, a process of socialization which begins at child birth and continues until death (Nuer religious expression: *"kuoth päle täth ran ε cε liu"*). Education is an influence consciously directed at adjusting thought, feeling and other forms of bchaviours and the experiences which molds attitudes and determine the conduct of both the child and the adult (Ayayo, 1976). This is the Nuer belief which specifies that education is spread throughout all stages of life that must appear, in some form, as described in this text. It is necessary to establish and how education is transferred to who and by whom it is connected and the content of what is being communicated.

Methods of communication are both plentiful and countless some of which include; means by which understanding is conveyed individual to another within a given cultural area. Among the Nuer we can determine two categories of techniques for communication: the primary techniques include language; signs, proverbs, idiom, gesture, stories, riddles and observation. The secondary techniques arc more modern and include printing, telephone, figures and so on. The latter category will not be considered here, since they were not familiar to a preliterate society. The significance of communication in philosophy and normative premises may be administrated in several ways. First, the members of a preliterate traditional society became aware of group identity and values that served as guides to their cultural behaviour. These were learnt through folk stories, past heroes, and past behaviors and institutions that existed in the past society. Second, the means and techniques of planting ideologic in the heart of the microbars of the society word dependent upon communication developed by a dominant cultural group in that society. Communications which carry ethical and ideological convictions may also carry punishments to those violating them. Some punishments were banishment, physical and mental pain, loss of prestige or destruction.

In the Nuer old-style form of education, the verbal symbols, became the chief means of expressing concepts. Yet some were not always necessarily verbalized. Symbols in the form of signs, such as nodding and shaking the head, waving, calling by hand signal were used very effectively. Anything symbols or signs used, they were used to transfer beliefs, norms, values and knowledge from one person to another, and from old to young. Symbolic learning was the medium through which the Nuer society brought together its members. In the plenary stage, members of a family learnt their obligations in the up longing of the younger generation. At the clan and sectional levels, they tended to share the same emotional states. This learning begins at home through intimate contact with parents and children. Parents teach their children what they have learnt from their own parents and grandparents and add to their experience as better guardians. These are Nuer societal patterns continuously repeated due to the ancestors of its members having built them in an orderly consistent system of living. The society's patterns are the result of practical education over a long period of time. Society counsels' parents to follow their duty of bringing up the younger generation to acquire the ancestors' culture, beliefs, and pattern. Let me spell out some specific functions of education in the traditional society before concrete aspects of the Nuer system of education.

Function of indigenous education

Education is essential as a form of social control in a traditional society due to the existence of a uniform system of education. That is, common polices exist as regards giving instructions that must be accepted. Education was to promote unity by emphasizing respect of the system, i.e., respect of age certainly creates a smooth running of a relationship for the sake of unity, and purposive actions of agreed values and norms. The traditional education stresses the common responsibility for youth by the elders; in turn due respect must be communicated, not only to the parents, but to all who undertake responsibilities, the lineage members, clan, and the tribe. Thus, kinship ties are strengthened throughout the clan so that no person will marry anyone who is considered to be related by kinship. Education was therefore essential for family life, and Kinship ties linking them with the clan, the religion of the clan and of the tribe were always congruent. The Nuer religious observations did not creat rigid rules that are impossible to attain and we find that there is always a solution to the problem. The importance of traditional education is heavily stressed from childhood and all that follows is built upon childhood education. It is this that has made preliterate societies what they are, and makes the difference between traditional education and formal education gained at school. Formal education gained at school is but a small factor in the development of manhood in the society. This may be stressed by the fact that formal school education very rarely teaches nonnative rules, beliefs and behaviour. We never come across, for examples, rules of respect to elders, rules that teach do not kill, tell lies, and so on, unless one is in a religious class or church, but all these rules are produced by traditional education, at all levels and in everyday instruction. I intend to call traditional education a "normative education" because it puts normative beliefs into the minds of the young members of the society.

Normative education

We have already noticed that normative beliefs have the responsibility for enforcing group values. Ayayo (1976), describes normative education as that stimulates sentimental beliefs which validates norms and customs. It teaches those desirable things society ought to do or to avoid doing certain things that are defined by the customs in a prescribed manner. It teaches normative rules, so that the purposes of the society may not be submerged by the actions of its members. The long-term effect of normative education in the traditional society appears effective where a prison system does not exist. Such as was the Nuer society before government chiefs were introduced in 1930s. Normative education was a means of social control by which individual members or a group of the clan induced to conform to the Nuer traditional conduct as represented by their traditional heroes. The significance of institution shapes the behaviour of the members depending largely upon the cultural educational setting; as Ayayo (1976). That is, the purpose of education or its content, and the rigidity of the system in the traditional ways of governing the societies.

Purpose of indigenous education

The aims of education in the traditional society are very wide-ranging and a child is expected to have covered all that his/her culture provides by the time he/she has aged (Ayayo, 1976). But a society, such as that of the Nuer discuss in this text, restrict some types of education for others. Here, some professions are passed on from generation to generation and therefore education in some cases is not open to all. For example, the blacksmith (*bel*) educates his son or other close relatives who will take over the workshop, but it is not given to children who are not members of the block front clan. Similarly, the knowledge required to a medicine man and to treat illnesses is not conveyed to all people. The Nuer, for example, believe that certain skills can only be inherited and that education alone may not be enough without the following aims:

The first purpose of Nuer traditional education provides a practical education which enables a Nuer child and later as a grownup person, to assist in the production of material wealth. A second purpose of education is to provide a child with the traditions, customize and the history of his ancestors. A third purpose is to give knowledge of an inner life, which only a few may be able to receive by veil true of their relationship to those whose ancestors possessed that knowledge. And lastly, is to maintain the Nuer ways of life, respect, honors and to keep the identity of the group wherever one may be. Learning that encourages personal independence naturally does not preach rigid group corporation. The form of strong group conformity is attained by a fair leadership, which Ayayo (1976), stresses that education demanded respect at all levels, the respect for elders becomes the driving force.

The concept of respect for elders among the Nuer is a limitless. It is not between a child and a grown-up person, rather it is hierarchical for all living members of the society and also for the dead. In the Nuer tradition, a child may not call his parents, grandparents or any other elder person by their names. This would be regarded as bad-mannered. Language used by children in conversation with elderly persons is mindful and must be much polite and polished than the language they use with contemporaries. In eating cow's meat, for example, respect of age and social status is strictly maintained. Some parts of the meat shall be eaten by certain persons but not by the others because of their age, sex, or social status. This hierarchical juncture strongly influences the arrangement of houses, villages, the position of sitting at ritual ceremonies, sacrifices, and even at the beer party. The oldest member of the family leads the group, unless proved to be traditionally and customarily unfit to be a leader. The senior member of the family, clan, sub-tribe of tribe whose conduct has been outstanding may become a folk hero. In the world of spirits, the Nuer believe that, likewise, they are also allocated according to age status, and the position occupied in life on earth.

Being taught respect directly calls for positions of prestige and honour, which must be conferred to certain members by virtue of their age, birth, seniority, wealth or of their function as members of the society. According to the Nuer rules of respect of age, a child may not tell an old person directly that "you are a louse" or that "you lie". Nor may a child say this to his parents or any other older than himself, even if he is certain that the old person is lying. Such a child will certainly be disciplined for such disrespect. He/she may however, say this to his/her contemporaries and juniors. The principles and aliens of education advocated by educators are the acceptably forms of principles of the society.

Apprenticeship for production skills

The education of technology of production among the Nuer is open to all children and is stressed according to gender: hence some duties are performed by men, some by women, and others are jointly performed (Ayayo, 1976). However the training of iron working is quite different from general education only given to male children among the Nuer. In the first place, it is given only to a member of the blacksmith (*bell*) clan who usually attends blacksmith workshop. Particularly, attention is paid to one of the children selected among several brothers because of his commitment to learning iron work. The education of smithing and smelting is a long process typically a boy begins by working the bellows for his elder smith. Throughout childhood, a boy learns the actual work, particularly the simpler tasks. However, he is not given the opportunity to work in his own workshop before he becomes a mature person. During this period, a boy learns to work some simple implements for example, making knives, (*ŋoamni*) using small pieces of leftover irons and fixing handles. He is introduced to various techniques of smithing, learning through observation and participation; verbal rites are linked with the secrets of iron production. He must dedicate his skill to the ancestral spirit of the black smith clan. And sacrifices offered for the ancestral spirit of the clan, and also for the elders who communicate with him. This further indicates that the art and knowledge of smithing and smelting has been handed down in the clan throughout the generations. The term "hammer" (*dei*) is from time immemorial used by Nuer Prophets like Ngundëŋ Bong he referred to Anyuak's blacksmith named Owar Worogol who the Nuer spell (*Wäär Joguol*) who made (constructed) Ngundɛŋ's Brass Pipe (*Tony Läŋ*), that implies an oath taking as a graduation after many years of mystical learning. It was because of this Ngundëŋ was said to have blessed and anointed an Anyuak black smith with oil- butter (*lïëth*) putting it around his mouth.

A similar pattern of training can be observed in pottery work: mostly done by girls. A daughter of a potter learns from her mother and takes over the pottery works after many years of practical training. She does not begin to make her own pots until when she becomes mature enough to handle issues. Also, the coaching of traditional medicines is given with best memory to both men and women. Children learn from their parents who are specialists in this field and show them all medicines and diseases which they cure before they pass on. The procedure is that whenever a patient comes to the medicine person (*Guän Wal*). The young person who is being trained sits beside his father or mother to hear the problem and may be requested to go to bring medicine, asked to mix it and prepares it before it is given to the patient. If a medicine specialist is a female, it is her daughter who inherits the skill of practicing medicine after her death. In this context, education and inheritance go together. These types of professions are what Ayayo (1976) referred to as "inherited professions".

Child punishment for non-conformity

Nuer children receive different forms of punishment for nonconformity including: physical penitent by whipping, defamation, temporary denial of sole premises or lights, psychological punishments, or denial of food. Some of the physical punishments are cruel, like beating to those who do not listen. During the first seven years, a child is under a strong parent's supervision and disciplinary actions. During this period, the parents apply physical punishment to the child. Elder brothers and sisters do the same punishment as well. The greater part of disciplinary action is composed of praise for exclamation of good deeds and rebuke for misbehavior. At this age, the language is used as a weapon of punishment for misbehaviors and as the acceptance of good behaviors from the child.

One of the most effective forms of punishment the Nuer use in the process of education is the "pejorative" song. A child, or a grown-up man, who breaks a custom is psychologically humiliated through the "derogative " songs. Should a man steal, for example, some fish, or a grown-up lili or man goes into the kitchen to steal food, a song is composed a gainst that person which will be spread all over the clan and beyond by different actors. Young girls and boys expose these songs throughout their playing games. The huge songs are sung in the fields, by a river or in the forest during outdoor activates. The girls may sing them to convey the song to other girls across the clan and through the whole Nuer land, so that other youth who happened to hear the song elsewhere may echo to others. In this manner the names of the persons who violate the custom may spread throughout the society and beyond the community. The consequences of this song go beyond the psychological effect that they carry with them. If it concerns a grown-up unmarried man or girl, it may affect his or her getting a mate, since, as we shall discover in the Nuer marriage, anti-social behaviour may cause divorce or prevent a proposal. Other punishments for non-conformity to the education pattern may have included threats of magic and witchcraft, Adolescent boys and girls who did not obey the rules that they should not be out too late, may have been warned by a threat of encountering witchcraft. However, the concept of punishment by "derogative songs" is more effective, because adolescent boys and girls work very sensitive to ridicule by critic ion horn their own contemporaries, from strangers as well as from their own parents and relatives.

Punishment as absorbed by Ayayo (1976) is not considered as cruelty, but may be conserved as once form of education. The overt techniques, such as exclusion or infliction of pain, cannot be indoctrinated in the Nuer system of education. The close cooperation, in the fun of strong kinship ties in a clan, creates social models of the tribe as a whole, which are persistently brought to the attention of the young and greatly influence the development of ideals, habits and other personality traits to the younger generation throughout the community. In a relatively homogeneous society that has common politics of education, members are closely related, so that psychological punishment is thus quite effective. The society does indeed care for its members with each person sharing another's problems; such characteristics do not appear in a more complex society The efficiency of education varies with changes in the social organization and life values of the group. In the present Nuer society, life values have unmultiplied, and this has medically reshaped the educational out-look.

In the traditional society, the education of custom was a powerful means of influencing the responses of individuals. What their heroes, or grandfathers did carried prestige and conviction. But even in contemporary Nuer life, it does not yet appear that the influence of tradition has been broken in such institutions as family life, religion, philosophical thinking and normative beliefs; ethical convictions have not significantly changed. This is so because much of which has been discussed in this work is still clear in the mind of most elderly Nuer people and they tried desperately to reinstitute them.

Changing Values in the society

Societal change starts with the children development in their new environment. Nuer children have been affected by the societal changes that have taken place in recent times such as we can see in the capital of South Sudan – Juba for example, where many Nuer children interact with other children in their playing games. Some of these changes have been necessitated by the rural urban migration, western education, Christianity and Islamic education. The school system in South Sudan is flexible where both languages, English and Arabic play major roles. This brought Nuer children into interaction with other communities. Many Nuer children thus find themselves in cosmopolitan set-ups. These new settings require modification of some elements as performed in the vernacular children's singing games, total improvisation of the singing games or even the performance of singing games that can communicate to children in a cosmopolitan setting. In many cosmopolitan areas, Nuer children form part of the performances and dramatization of various children's playing games. They join other children from other communities in performing urban children's playing games. These games are performed in English and Arabic in Juba and other big cities. Many of these games reveal how traditional Nuer values are undergoing change. Children engage in the playing games in groups within, schools, churches and even at the market as they disengage themselves from adults and creatively dramatize in their own activities. In their performances, it is evident that children do not discriminate, they play as friends, without the prejudice that many adults harbour on other communities. Even when alone, Nuer children carry on with various performances that reflect the urban influence, and also the new values emerging from their involvement with other children, western education, the electronic media, Christianity and Islam. In this new situation, children show their understanding of the immediate environment and also their imitation of the same. The performance requires a lot of creativity as the participants are expected to think of something they have experienced in the urban set up. When they go back to their rural setting in villages, they are already different people with different knowledge and understanding.

Though the Nuer people live in close-knit clan system based on the value of communality, many of them have now interacted with other communities and have also been influenced by other traditions and cultures such as; Christianity, Islam and western education referred to earlier. Let's take Juba as cosmopolitan for example. When Nuer children interact with other children in their playing games, they would imitate the adult world as they sing and entertain themselves during their cultural activities. Their playing games would reflect the aesthetics and cultural values of the Nuer people. These cultural values have however, been influenced by many factors. A strong participation in Nuer children revealed that Nuer children as they, play and dramatize in their mother-tongue, their games cannot really be said to be exclusive to the Nuer world only. These other worlds are evident to the fact that Nuer children's games are self-motivated and flexible, able to comment on changing values in the wider Nuer society. Their games reflect the changing socio-economic and other issues in the child's environment. Some of these issues may include: life styles, religion and education.

Value of Formal Education

Traditionally, the Nuer people had in the past informal type of education in which the children were trained through oral narratives and also as apprentices to adults who taught them skills like fishing, swimming, wood work, farming and others. However, with the advent of formal education as a result of colonization and western and Arabic education, the Nuer first hardly accepted these new education models for the boys and rejected their girls going to schools. Among the Nuer people, girls were for a long time sidelined when it came to formal education. Indeed, many girls were stopped from going to school and forced into early marriages. Nuer reservations were associated education with prostitution, colonization and exploitation of the inhabitants and it was also meant to condition the natives to hate themselves and even their culture. It was until recently, that the Nuer realized these values of formal education with its benefits. Nowadays, Nuer children start criticizing their 'parents' for trying to stop them from acquiring formal education. Nevertheless, given that many traditional Nilotic societies were patriarchal, there was a lot of gender imbalance in the reception of this formal education. Though, this trend has now changed as the government has placed a policy: that a girl child is encouraged to acquire formal education and move away from the traditional domestic chores.

Many Nuer girls have now acquired certificates so as to cope with the fast-changing society. This challenge was ironical and revealed that the discrimination of the Nuer girls was real and must be averted so as to empower them through formal education. The significance of formal education similar to that of the Nuer was emphasized by Weche (2009), citing Luo children's singing games in Kenya; describing how the children observed and learn in their new environment. The changing values in Luo children's singing games show that children are keen observers of what is happening around them. Their singing games also reveal that children's literature is dynamic and reflects the values of the macro society in which children live (Weche, 2009). The values dramatized and performed in their singing games cannot therefore be divorced from the norms, expectations, changing values and the aesthetics of their community in which the Nuer people of South Sudan could learn from.

Language policy conundrum in South Sudan

South Sudan, like many newly independent African states, has had to make very difficult choices in language policy owing to the intricate setup of multi-culturalism and multilingualism, factors emanating from the diverse ethnic and linguistic groups enforced by colonial rule. The South Sudan situation is unique due to double triple colonialism under Arabs, British and the Islamic north administration of the Sudan state. Add to several wars, firstly to liberate the south and internal conflicts that have displaced communities pushing a large population out of the country.

Within those years spanning decades, several policies favoured English and Arabic without any regard to about 64 spoken indigenous languages in the south. The school system has never adopted UNESCO recommendation in 1953 that "It is axiomatic that the best medium for teaching a child is his mother tongue. Psychologically, it is the system of meaningful signs that in his mind works automatically for expression and understanding. Sociologically, it is a means of identification among the members of the community to which he belongs. Educationally, he learns more quickly through it than through an unfamiliar linguistic medium (UNESCO, 2003)". African countries that got their independence earlier beginning with Sudan 1956 have been providing education to children in primary schools in indigenous languages with earliest transition to the preferred foreign languages at grade four.

When some Nilotic languages were introduced earlier by the missionaries and the colonial administration in Sudan the aim was to replace some of the functions of Arabic which had taken root in the Southern Sudan during the Turko-Egyptian and Mahadiya periods. Rather than support for allowing the indigenous languages, the action brought the people together through languages situation in pre- and post-colonial South Sudan and it is this reason that the policy of local languages empowerment was reversed at independence in 1956, but Sudan government favoured Arabic language. The use of Nilotic languages at the time, appeals for the creation of a new and favourable political climate to enhance the development of Nilotic languages based on their common origin. The language policies were influenced by colonial experiences which were to a large extent determined by: the missionaries, colonial administrators and post- colonial governments.

In the Southern Sudan, work on the local languages started as early as 1848 and continued until the mid-1930s. In 1928 the colonial government gave support to this policy of vernacular language empowerment by recognizing the use of the local languages in administration and in education. Six languages were selected for this purpose: Bari, Shilluk, Dinka, Zande, Nuer and Lotuho (Prah, 2000). The local languages and English were employed to replace some of the functions of Arabic which had taken root in the Southern Sudan as a language of trade during the Turko- Egyptian and Mahadiya eras. The development of the local languages was encouraged and actively supported first by the missionaries then later on by the colonial government. The missionaries found the local languages to be effective for their religious work. Early work on the local languages was devoted to translating the Bible. Eventually, dictionaries such as Nuer dictionary published in 1950s and other literacy materials for education were transliterated. However, this policy of vernacular empowerment was reversed at independence in 1956 in favour of Arabic. The language policy of the Sudanese government since 1956 has been to deny that languages other than the Arabic language existing in the country.

The government only grudgingly admits that there are African languages spoken in the South of the country but then does everything in her power to discourage their use in any meaningful context. This was a direct reversal of British colonial policy in the Sudan which recognized the use of the local languages in administration and education in the South. The post-colonial Sudanese government felt the development of the African languages was detrimental to

National Unity. For the sake of unity and stability and national integration, the North felt the country needed one language (Arabic) which was to be used in all areas of national lifecycle. As early as 1904 the governor-general of Sudan declared that there was a need for only some 'moderately education Blacks' to fill minor official post in the South. The government invested very little in education sector in the southern region, which was subcontracted to missionary societies. Unlike the education policy heavily invested in the Northern provinces. Generally, education policy for the South focused mainly on vernacular education as a barrier to' detribalization. The policy aims to keep southern people backwards as government's education was directed to making the individual south Sudanese to learn their own dialects and send back to their villages to live in normal environment with no advance education. This restrictive method did not give an opportunity for southern students to graduate to advance levels of schooling. With exception of only a small number attended the Church-run Intermediate Schools where instruction was in English and where the first cadre of southern teachers, clerical staff, and junior administrators were trained (Johnson, 2016). Not all administrators agreed with the limitations of southern policy. The emphasis on vernacular education was already being reversed educational policy in the South was recognized in Khartoum even before the end of World War Two. Throughout the early 1940s administrators in the south were becoming more vocally critical of the lack of development policies for their provinces. Pressure from within administration weakened southern policy, s rationale, but its final demise was brought about by the postwar challenges of Egyptian and northern Sudanese nationalism. Egypt's attempt to reassert its sovereignty over the whole of Sudan forced British administrators into an uneasy alliance with the anti-Egyptian faction of northern Sudanese nationalists. The ramifications of Anglo-Egyptian rivalry for the support of Sudanese political factions would bring southern Sudanese into the center of Sudanese political life from which they had been excluded. The South where African languages are spoken went to war with the North in 1955 which dragged on until 1972. There was an attempt in the 1950s and early 1960s to rewrite the local languages (especially those which were selected for educational purposes) from roman- based to a modified Arabic script. The resentment and resistance engendered by this move was one of the causes that led to the first war which lasted for seventeen years (1955-1972), with Addis Ababa Accord that temporarily ended the conflict. These examples show that political intervention can play a positive or a negative role in the development of languages.

The South Sudanese including the Nuer, aware about the policies of the government, viewed these with skepticism, arguing that it would have negative implications on non–Muslims. They were convinced that the powers that Government entrusted to the Islamist politicians led by Hassan al-Turabi was effectively putting an end to Addis Ababa Accord and threatening the regions' rights granted to the South in the 1973 Constitution. By 1981 there was no Southerner in the Numeiri cabinet and the South was thus deprived of a voice to argue their case against the process of establishing an Islamic State which eventually happened in 2002. This was the impassioned situation in which the successive governments in Sudan determined to take drastic action against the Christian south by introducing such policies in a multi-cultural state.

Through the colonial history, disrespect for African culture, with their fundamental values and related institutions, have been disrupted. Aspect of these foreign interventions led to domination and conflicts which consequently affected cultural behaviours of the indigenous Nuer people.

CHAPTER EIGHT:
ECONOMY

The sources of Wealth

Being a rich person among the Nuer primarily meant having many cattle as well as many wives and children. Wealth is also inherited from the parents' male line. It carries with it generosity, humility and care for others in need. Respect for both men and women depended very much on having many children. As one researcher noted, without having "fashioned", one could certainly not be a respected person in the community (Ojijo 2012). It is seen as the responsibility of a rich person to step in and help other families in need. The entire Nuer society is basically looking after each other. However, amassing wealth is not an aim. Although a man who owns a large herd of cattle may be coveted, his possession of numerous animals does not gather him any special privilege within the society. There is no special treatment for how one is treated because of their richness in cattle. Being rich does not qualify one to be a leader because it is a part of their role in the society particularly in kinship to do so particularly in economic marriage. As noted in the next section that deals with the centrality of cattle in Nuer economy. Cattle are not primarily kept for food, though the Nuer drink milk, an animal is only scarified at important festivities. Because of their location along the Nile and its availability, fish is an essential part of Nuer subsistence economy. Occasionally, hunting plays an important part of their food. In addition, subsistence farming of maize, sorghum, vegetables and millet are important parts of their diet. Most of the Nuer land is suitable for stock-breeding than agriculture: it is a flat, clayey, savannah nation that is parched and plain during the drought and easily flooded and covered in high grasses during the rainy seasons.

The importance of land

The Nuer cherish land in the following order: land for pasture, land for a village site and land for cultivation and for communal use. Different types of land have certain value utilized by the Nuer each time of the year. The, high land, ranges of higher, better-drained ground, provides for the permanent settlements mainly occupied during the rains from May to November. This period is used for the cultivation of staple crops such as sorghum, maize and tobacco and the few vegetables which some Nuer grow. In the past, the Nuer were unaware of the value of crop rotation, and do not use fertilizers such as cattle dungs and other manures which they could use to fertilize the soil; when the ground is exhausted. They simply abandon the land and move elsewhere, to reconstruct their houses and cattle-byres on a new location. There is therefore no high degree of durability of tenure, and no rigidity of rights in arable land (Howell, 2018). Any person and his family have the prescriptive right to use the land they have selected and cleared, due to the exclusion of every other person. Hence, the ownership of the land includes; high land, for cultivations and permanent settlements, intermediate, land for pasture usually in the early months of the dry season, for summer grazing (*toic*) and also these rights extent to fishing ground usually from January – April.

Before the Nuer were introduced to market economy the population was still under control. One person used to occupy as much area of land as he wishes, roughly one square mile or more, of which the land around the village was divided among his family members including; wives and sons for cultivation. The remaining was left for grazing cattle and other livestock around their homestead, although there is a common grazing area for all the community of the village. The importance of land used for cultivation was principally of subsistence value. Land in terms of agricultural products has only ' 'use value" and cattle stand for exchange value. When the land is valued in terms of pasture, it is not often the case that it is suitable for cultivation at the same time. A village site was also situated close to the water source or streams, but it is uncommon to find water in most of the areas in Nuer land particularly in Lɔu and Gaawɛ̈ɛr Nuer territories. The Nuer value land for grazing from a distance and also try to be able to see possible intruders. The Nuer value land most of their ancestors have fought and died for it. This to Nuer is the basic land right in the society. There is strongest assertion to land that one's ancestors have fought for and acquired it by conquest and blood. Nuer expansion to the eastern Nile in the 18th century see at that lance draws its value through blood when the Nuer were interacting with other ethnic communities such as the Dinka, Anywaa and Burun mentioned ealier in this text. This principle is extended in the belief that land now occupied by any particular (group) was fought for and conquered by the ancestors of its present-day members (Ayayo, 1976). Normative value of land is brought about by the shedding of blood and by kinship ties. Individual rights to land vary, but that domain of the grave of one's ancestor has the uppermost value and is untransferable.

Figure 9:8:ombination of the Nuer economy

Photos by: Gabriel Gai Riam

The implication of a mixed agriculture means of subsistence among the Nuer nowadays shows a practice of mixed economy. They are no longer considered to be a pastoral community, as members of the Nilotic pastoral society in the past. Agriculture and fishing later became part of their subsistence pattern particularly after migration and settlement in their current territories. In consideration of the theory of Nilotic migration, as advanced by historians, the Nilotes could also have been influenced by the agricultural life in the eastern regions. This shows how the three operators work in economic life of the Nuer society and the linking values between agriculture, livestock and fishing industries. The combination of these three modes of life can be assumed to have changed the Nuer society to some degree before outside modern developments were recognized. Nuer economy is therefore, based on a combination of cattle rearing, agriculture, fishing, gathering of wild fruits and hunting. Cattle are the most cherished possession because they are a source of food and is the most important social asset. Cows play an important role in rituals, institutions, customs and social behaviours.

Based on my experiences and interviewees I have had with some Nuer elders, the purpose of bloodletting is not perceived as parasitic to the animals. The reasons why the Nuer perform the operation is to supplement the available dietary supplies, especially in the dry season. Besides, bloodletting is a treatment regimen for sick, malnourished animals suffering from a condition called *noi*. The elders believe that bleeding cures a cow of unfitness by letting out the infected blood. These observations affirm the notion that the Nuer care for their livestock and do not slaughter their stock for food, except during epidemics. Pritchard noted the same that the usual occasions when the Nuer eat meat are during rituals. In such events, the festal character of rites gives them food its significance in the people's life. Since cattle are the most cherished possession because they provide food and are the most important social asset, it is easy to understand why they play an integral role in the Nuer life. A man establishes contact with the ghosts and spirits through his cattle, which are dedicated to the spirits of the lineages for the owner and of his wife and to any personal spirit that has at some time possessed either of them. Nuer may sanctify other animal to the ghosts of the dead, a mode keeping the link and way of meditating with the spirit.

Despite the importance of cattle among the Nuer, there are several inevitable problems related to owning of livestock. The animals have been the major cause of the conflicts among the community's different sub-groups and between the community and its neighbors. As noted earlier on, cattle are central in Nuer life and have been affecting the politics of contacts between them and with their nearby pastoralists. Cattle represent Nuer social, cultural and economic security, and therefore can be truly a source of conflict especially in the grazing places of the Upper-Nile and Bahr el Ghazal regions.

The attitude of Nuer and their relations with neighbouring peoples are influenced by their love of cattle and desire to acquire them. Nuer conflicts with Dinka and Murle communities have been about the raids of cattle and control of pastures. Each Nuer clan has its pastures and water-supplies, and political fission is closely related to distribution of natural resources. The ownership is generally expressed in clans and lineages. Disputes between clans are often about cattle. Livestock is used to compensate for any crime committed in which community social agents are involved. Their roles and responsibilities are observed and respected within the society. Key among these agents, are the; Leopard-skin chiefs, government appointed chiefs and Prophets who arbitrate in matters related to cattle. Others are ritual agents who intercede for the community in situations that demand the sacrifice of an ox or ram. An example of a ritual specialist is the *wut-hok,* whose spiritual power mainly focuses on cattle.

Indigenous methods of Agriculture
In addition to cattle rearing, the Nuer practice agriculture. Crops are grown in small quantities with little labour, using no fertilizers or crop rotation. In Nuer traditional rural settings, people till land using "hoes". Children observed what adult do in their daily activities. They play minor roles such as collecting grass that have been cleared or cut by the adults and removed them away from the fields. This agricultural practice often leaves the soils depleted. The main crops grown by the community include maize, sorghum, beans, vegetables, millet and tobacco. Traditionally, demand for food during periods of shortage was met by gathering wild fruits and fishing mentioned earlier on in this text.

 Recently, the Nuer have picked up trading as a form of subsistence. Such trends become important components of their economy besides rearing livestock and practicing agriculture. The goal for the community's economic activities is to satisfy families' immediate dietary needs and to accumulate wealth. The size of farm land belonging to each household depends on financial ability. On average, every household cultivates between two to three acres, mostly for subsistence consumption. When crops fail because of floods or drought, areas that have surplus harvests are often open to batter. While Nuer economy includes agriculture, soil in Nuerland is purely black, soggy clay. This type of soil could also be suitable for cotton farming for example, in western bank of the Nile and central Nuer, where cotton can be found grown in small scale for household use such as threads for sewing broken gourd, clothes and others cultural necessities. Agricultural practices in Nuer are characterized by the use of rudimentary tools. However, new implements such as ox plough and Tractors introduced by proceeds from relief aids agencies and government can now be spotted in the fields. Nuer children also reflect a movement away from traditional values to adoption of modern values including education rather than removing of grass in the fields.

Hunting as a cultural game and source of food supplement
Indigenous hunting ("*käk*") of wild animals was another important activity among the Nuer. It was to meet community needs, as well as for cultural pride. Hunting is performed by individual and also by large groups of people. Large game animals such as Elephants, Rhinos, Buffalo and Giraffe were hunted for their valuable parts such as, Elephant tusks, skins, Giraffe tail whisks (*miiy jual gueec*), Rhino horns and meat. There were indigenous rules and regulations governing hunting activity. For example, when an Elephant is felled and killed, the person who speared the Elephant first takes the right tusk and the second tusk goes to the second person. Similarly, in the case of buffalo, the hides and head go to the person who speared it first. The horns of Rhino are given to the person who first speared it and the tail is given in case of Giraffe. After instituting these simple procedures governing this habitual activity, the rest of

the animal is cut randomly by those present at the scene and other community members are invited to partake in the distribution of the animal's meat.

The custom of ritual sharing of meat, is so common among the Nuer. The sharing repasts are known to have had a religious character found among them: For example, the Nuer *gaatnäcä* clan owes a hind leg (*ham*) to the Thiang clan and a foreleg (Jëar) to the Jimɛn clan and the *gaat Buli* clan etc. The *Jibothni* are the people who cut the scrotum of animals. Each family also has its *gwän bothni,* a detached relative in charge of ritual, particularly the slaughtering (killing) of animal. This person who slaughters (*Ji̱eng*) and skinned the animal receives a fix amount of meat. The rest of the meat is rightly divided as follows: head (*wic*) and hump (*bom*) liver (*cueny*) for elderly people, ribs for married young ladies (*nyer*) and the boys receive *mëaan* (rectum) and so on. The order in which the parts of the animals were shared during hunting expeditions is a cultural practice that was followed in post independence struggles when positions of leadership were shared in line with individual and community contribution at the time.

This custom of sharing among the Nuer extends to situations when people are experiencing severe starvation caused by catastrophe such as; famine, drought and flood resulting to hunger, affecting the families especially the children. In Nuer culture, the person who is badly affected and in need of food, would just go to a neighbour or relative who has livestock , pick a cow without permission, kills it, to rescue his/her family from dying of hunger. The person whose animal has been taken neither quarrel nor file a case against that individual who has taken the animal without first asking for help. The mater is amicably settled latter when this period of adversity has ended. This was one of the good humanitarian gesture the Nuer self-governance permitted in the past. These unique functions has changed gradually over the years. New rules and regulations instituted.

Nowadays with availability of fire arms in the hands of indigenous young people, the trends of killing endangered species has increased. In recent past however, old indigenous method of killing animals randomly has changed and new rules and regulations governing animal hunting have been introduced by the government led by the National Ministry of Wildlife Conservation and Tourism, Republic of South Sudan. In addition, no Nuer person nowadays can take and kill sombody's animal without permission just because of hunger; the laws do not permit. Nevertheless, with current conflicts in the country, particularly in the Nuer Nation, these rules are facing myriads of challenges. For example, lack of present of law enforcement agencies in many parts of Nuerland and National Game Reserves among others are risk to pouching.

Fishing for life sustenance
Changing values in the Nuer society range from human interaction to modern fishing techniques of different kinds. Traditionally, the Nuer people were fishermen and had an attraction to the rivers and the lakes. Such like River Nile, Sobat River, Akobo River and Lake No, they used traditional methods of fishing. In recent times changing methods in this fishing industry have taken shape. Introduction of fishing hooks and nets and training are quite common. Fishing boats and speed boats are used, making it possible for surplus fish to the

markets. Here we can see an overt revelation of some cultural practices. These attribute changes to various factors including learning new techniques, preparation and urbanization is becoming real in modern Nuer society. The changing values within the society play a crucial role in acquiring new methods of fishing, meaning evolution of Nuer cultural practices. This adaptation reveals the community's changing values on using fishing methods: fishing gears, hooks, modern canoes and Speed Boats. This industry has now gained attractiveness among the Nuer fishermen along the River Nile and other tributaries.

The centrality of cattle in Nuer economy
The Nuer always talk about their livestock, mainly cattle, which they include in their folklore, marriage practices, religious ceremonies, and relations with their neighbors. Nuer life revolves around cattle, which makes them pastoralists. Nonetheless they sometimes resort to horticulture, especially when their cattle are endangered by diseases. This love for cattle is so much so that the young men often get nicknames coinciding with the colours of their favourite oxen. Pritchard (1940) noted that the importance of cattle in Nuer life and thought is demonstrated in their personal names. They form their children's names from the biological features of the cattle (Pritchard, 1940). Nearly all Nuer men are named after their cattle. Children in their playing games usually chose the name of their favorite cattle based on the form and color of an ox. Young girls are named after the cows that they milk as a signed of their oneness with the cows and love. The importance of cattle is reflected in naming people. The community use color and shape of their animals to name children and men, such as "*makuac*'' a white ox with black spots, *Kuechärä* (black) with white spot on the forehead, *chotborä* (hornless white cow or bull), *tuong boor* (white horns), *chär* (black) and so on. Similarly, their dinka neighbours use cow or ox color to name their children as well. That reveals cultural closeness of the two Nilotic communities. Possessing many cattle adds to one's prestige, since cattle wealth is a marker of favorability among the Nuer. They primarily raise and herds cattle which is central to many aspects of in their daily life. Cattle play a central role in Nuer culture serving not only as a food, but also representing a symbol of wealth, social status and religious significance. Both Nuer men and women always prefer to be called by their favorite oxen or cattle (s (see Figure 7)howing Nuer oneness with the animals.

Figur 9 |0: Picture showing Nuer oneness with animals

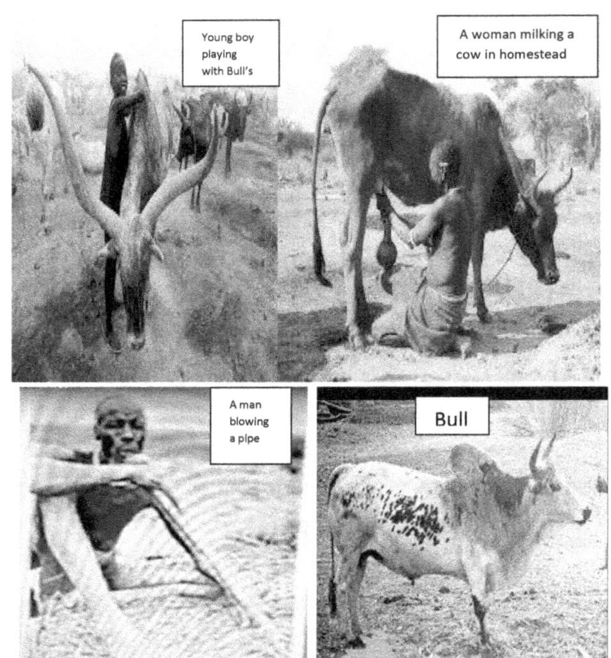

The Nuer do not just slaughter (kill) cattle for nothing nor slaughter animals solely because of the desire to eat meat. As Hutchinson (1996) noted what appears to be an ironic twist to the Nuer traditions concerning the meaning of the expression *"ca yang näk Lorä bang"*, which loosely translates to "a cow is never slaughtered for nothing." During the 1930s this expression was universally invoked by the Nuer to affirm their rejection of the nonsacrificial slaughtering of cattle and other livestock. There is indeed a very strong feeling amounting to a moral injunction that domestic animals must not be slaughtered except in sacrifice (Hutchinson, 1996). She also noted that trade and increasing Christian evangelization happened among the Nuer between the 1970s and the 1980s, and probably is the reason the expression; *ca yaŋ näk Lorä baŋ* is perceived differently. Nuer Christian converts considered the act of killing cattle as negative and linked it to one of the Ten Commandments *"Thou shalt not kill"* and belittling the significance of sacrifices in Nuer traditions. There is also the fear of the ox's spirit visiting a curse on any person who slaughters it without ritual intent, aiming only to use it for food. The Nuer believe that a cow should not be simply slaughtered except as a sacrifice to the gods, the spirits and the ancestors. It must be emphasized that Nuer are basically a pastoral society, since they were originally Nilotic society that mainly depend on cattle and other livestock like goats and sheep. Though the Nuer now cultivate more, and some less, according to their present ecological setting, soil conditions and rainfall, as well as population densities which in some regions regulate the cattle wealth, they still regard that agriculture must be mixed with cattle rearing. This incentive of cultivation was forced upon them by the poverty of cattle. This was and still so when I talked to many community leaders who stressed their old days as amusing, when cattle were still abundant.

The Nuer were and still dependent on cattle for most of the lives socio-economic and cultural necessities, many of which cattle still fulfil, but cattle there were, and still are, being possessed for prestige. The Nuer sometimes risk their lives in defense of their cattle against neighbors and wild animals that may attempt and in search for them if they get lost. The attitude of the early pastoral Nuer and their relations with neighboring people has been much influenced in different ways. First, their love ideology of exogamous marriage which allow cattle to be transferred outside their community groups to neighboring communities, some of which were originally considered as foes; second, their love for kingship motivated the transfer of their most beloved possessions to them to establish peace. If this was not achieved, their love of cattle and desire to acquire them generated serious conflict with their neighbors.

Quarrels between families or lineages are very often about cattle: For example, cattle may eat someone else crops, some compensation would be paid for as well as cattle of the bridal wealth that have not been paid. Cattle, were compensation for loss of life or limb or broken leg. Ritual agents in situations demanding sacrifice are spiritual leaders and diviners. The community leaders were often called to discuss cases where cattle and land issues were involved. Cattle were owned by families, and the head of the homestead had full rights of disposal over the herd, through obligations of marrying a wife to each son controlled his misuse of cattle. Sons, marry in order of seniority, each marries with cows from the herd assigned to him by the father. But contributions from other relatives may also take place. If the head of the homestead dies before any of the sons become married, his brother becomes the protector of the family and its cattle and the birth of the first child, he can take the leadership of the family and be responsible for his younger brothers until they are all married. The senior son will then take responsibility for the distribution of cattle among other youngsters and it will be his obligation to see that each unmarried sons gets married by the cattle from the head. This rule is observed and respected by all the family.

Despite the love of cattle by the Nuer, however, sheep and goats are used for sacrifices at ceremonies. The community believes that certain ghosts and spirits should be appeased as a matter of priority. Such rituals justify the occasional slaughter of animals. In most cases, oxen and barren heifers are slaughtered during sacrifices. However, productive cows could be sacrificed in ritual rites related to the death of female member. In certain instances, lactating cows could be slaughtered if an old grandmother passed on.

Evans-Pritchard who had written extensively about the Nuer observed that most people are interested in festival events than religious rites and that the Nuer are rich in cattle, and have a startling reputation of being ashamed for killing oxen for meat. The community advocates that people should not slaughter an ox solely for food unless in cases where there is severe famine. Though the Nuer do not slaughter for the sake of meat, an animal that succumbs to death due to natural reasons is eaten. The cattle's outward features such as the coloration and shape of horns are significant. However, size of the animal is the most important attribute. The Nuer admire a large hump (*bom*) which wobbles when the animal walks, and often manipulate the hump at birth to accentuate the feature (Pritchard, 1956).

Cattle also provide secondary products used for various purposes. Skins are used as beds, sleeping mats, and cord for tethering, leather collars for oxen, and making of drums. The community uses hides to manufacture of pipes and snuff-containers. The scrotal sacks of the Bulls are made into bags to carry tobacco, spoons, and other small objects. Tail hairs are made into tassels used by girls as dance ornaments and to decorate the horns of favorite oxen. The cows' horns are cut into spoons and used to make harpoons. Dung is used as fuel and for plastering walls, floors, and the exterior walls of the straw huts in cattle camps. Dry cow dung (*wär*) is also used to protect the cattle themselves by burning it to produce smoke keeping insects such like tsetse flies away to prevent diseases. The ashes of burnt cow dung (*puoh*) are rubbed over men's' bodies, used to dye and for straightening the hair. Dung ash is also used as a mouth wash, tooth powder, and to prepare sleeping-skins and leather bags. It is also serving various purposes during rituals. The urine (*këëth*) is an ingredient during the milk churning and cheese making process.

The skins (*kol*) of sheep and goats are worn as loin garments by married women and as rugs for sitting. They can also be made into bags for storing tobacco and millet, or cut into strips tied round their ankles by youths when dancing. The Nuer traditional norms and practices have undergone some transformation recently. However, cattle remain the role measure of the community's wealth, and a proper understanding of the Nuer social life is only possible if you understand the community's relationship with cattle.

Like other Nilotic pastoralist such as the Murle, Dinka and Mundari, cattle provide other dietary products to the Nuer. Evans Pritchard recognizes the importance of Nuer as cattle owners, comparing them to the *Bedouin Arabs* who have been called the *parasite of the camel*. Justifiably, the Nuer can also be called the *parasite of the cow*. However, Pritchard clarifies that this comparison between the Bedouin Arabs and the Nuer does not amount to the Nuer being parasites of their cattle in the real sense. The Nuer extract blood from the necks of their cows to supplement their diet and cure the animal. The process of drawing blood from an animal's veins using a shape knife consists of tying a cord tightly round a cow's neck so that the veins stand out, then piercing (*bär*) one of the veins with a small knife (*ngom*). The knife is bound with cord or grass to prevent a deep entry into the veins of the cow. The blood of the cow spurts out into a large gourd, suppose it is meant for dietary supplement otherwise it pours to the ground if the operation was for the purpose of treating the animal only. Upon completing the process, the cord is loosened and dung smeared over the wound to curtail further blood flow.

In recent times however, it has been observed that more Nuer are now slaughtering their livestock for commercial purposes to diversify income and address food inadequacy brought about by natural and manmade disasters such as floods, famine and wars. Almost every Nuer cultural practice and social activities relates to livestock. The circulation of cattle between the members of lineage increased key relations. Cattle and other types of livestock such as goats and sheep have special position in religious ceremonies. Animals are sacrificed to treat illness as a way of praying to God to bring rain, make the lands fertile and provide a good harvest as well as appeasing the ancestors. Livestock is the Nuer currency used in trading transaction. Although the community's economy is based on the combination of cattle herding, horticultural processes, and fishing, pastoralism takes precedence because it provides daily nutrition and contributes to the general social societal value in other aspects of life.

Cross border trade

In her research work, Hutchinson (1996), has noted that Nuer trading activities demand that they make bi-annual relocations between relatively permanent, wet-season settlements scattered across territory occupying about 25,000 square miles of marsh-laden savannah land and the more condensed temporary dry-season settlements. Cattle rearing and fishing activities were practiced along the major tributaries of the Nile (Hutchinson, 1996). Although there were few "Arabs' merchants coming to the region at the time, offering supplies such as fishing gears, boats, hoes and metallic items in exchange for hides, grains/sorghum and goats. These goods did not impress the Nuer. The impact of the goods on the community's economy was very insignificant. The Nuer were unfamiliar with currency market exchange concepts at the time of their interaction with Arabs. The Nuer interaction and "Arab" traders was mutual and not impersonal transactions at the time. In these connections, the concept of price did not play direct part in the trading activities.

The purpose of the economy is to produce goods and services and distribute them through a well-functioning price mechanism. In an ideal market system, a coherent economy abides by working rules and regulations. Unfortunately, such a system was lacking in the Nuer subsistence economy. However, their foreign traders had knowledge of price mechanisms and took advantage of the Nuer traditional trade system its people's ignorance to short change them.

In the past, the Nuer used to practice barter's system (commodity exchange) of goods and services. People who produce surplus foods could exchange it for livestock. For example, surplus grains or sorghum could be exchanged for a cow, goat, or any other such item that one felt deficient in. When other cultures introduced the Nuer to items such as sugar, salts, clothes, medicine and soap, the community felt compelled to acquire them through the only means they had; batter exchange system. The easier way was to buy those goods to sell livestock in the city to get cash. However, selling cattle was culturally shameful at the time. It took the action of the British Colonial Government imposing a poll tax and insisting that the levy be paid in cash that the Nuer began to sell their livestock. Arab's traders came into Nuerland to sell goods, and to open shops. In doing so, they imported grains from North Sudan to the nearby markets. The extension of trade introduced a cross-section of the Nuer community to leap into trading. The local traders started by selling oxen in the city to buy the Arab goods for their primary use.

In the later 20th century, few Nuer traders managed to enter the cattle export market and traded cattle up to north Sudan mainly Kosti and Khartoum. As noted by Johnson (2016), it was the trade in cattle, even more than the introduction of money, that prompted ruptures and debates among the Nuer about the meaning and power of money including over Nuer social and political relationships. The selling of cattle for money prompted new questions about the social convertibility of cattle to money (Johnson, 2016). The demand for money slowly grew as from the 1940s in the context of Anglo-Egyptian Condominium period which was linked to the government, s introduction of cattle auctions and Nuer desires to be buyers in these markets. From the 1950s, the government also recruited Nuer men to work on large cotton plantations in the north Sudan as migrant labour that has been part of their lives ever since and a general trend towards the adoption of money. Yet, money still lacked blood as it could not tie people together in the way that cattle use to do. The kind of loyalties that could be created through the exchange of money was seen by many Nuer to be weak in contrast to relationships built on the exchange of cattle. In those early days as well as the current times, grain and other food items were exchanged for cattle, other animal stock, and other commodities, and were considerable trade, which increased in volume in years of famine. Currently, with the introduction of a money economy, grain is bought with cash either from other Nuer, neighbouring communities or from Arab merchants, who subsidized by the government, regularly to import huge amounts to meet local shortages.

In the early 1960s, a major change has occurred: the Nuer found opportunities for hard labor in construction projects especially in the then northern Sudan. The youth traveled to work in agricultural farms and construction projects during the dry seasons. Much of the money they earned was used to buy basic supplies and cows. In addition to their involvement in modern trade, the Nuer produced a variety of personal items such as clay pots, smooth mugs, decorated kitchenware, and smart baskets, and papyrus mats. They exchanged these goods for items they lacked at home. The Nuer economy changed because of an increased use of fiat. Micro economic activities evolved as a result. By 1960s, the Nuer younger generation embarked on the path to gain formal education putting them above some economic activities such like skill labor, masonry, welding, building and construction work in north Sudan.

During and after the civil wars periods (1955- 1972 and 1983- 2005), the Nuer economy has been greatly affected. The civil wars have displaced a large population from their ancestral land making them migrated to different regions and the diaspora as refugees and also internally displaced persons (IDPs). Previously as noted ealier in the 1960s through their skill labor, they then began accepting cash currency into their economy. The impact of this civil wars have changed the dynamics of their indigenous ways of trade which was mainly centered round cattle. In respond to these changes, Nuer indigenous cattle economy has been transformed into modern cash transactions. Presently, each type of cattle is titled according to how they are acquired in case of marriage such as: "the cattle of money" which nowadays called lame cattle (*Yok ti duänyni* - purchased with cash currency) and "the cattle of girls/daughters" (bride wealth). These as noted above, as social changes and cultural developments were due to the impact of civil wars that have torn the country apart and mark off Nuer moral values less absolute limitations of behaviour.

CHAPTER NINE:
NUER ETHICAL AND MORAL VALUES

Pillars of the nation's integrity

Morality is a special set of values that mark off more or less absolute limitations of behaviours. It includes such basic rules as "do" and "don't" as well as general system of duties and obligations in society. Morality is sometimes summarized as the list of those actions that people ought to do or refrain from doing. It is only a small part of ethics, however, the rules and rituals that define society and living well within it are far more extensive than the limitations of morality. Morality may set the guidelines and especially mark off what actions are utterly forbidden, but it is ethics that more generally sets positive goals and defines the meaning of life (Solomon and Clancy, 2004). Furthest studies of Nilotic peoples throughout South Sudan have wrapped their moral values differently. For example, Dinka believe *nhialic* (God) and in Shilluk *Jwok* (God) while Anyuak too call God *nyikang*. All these ethnic communities have different priests and pillars concerned with their welfare. The Nuer have their moral thoughts refer to, as moral values which sustain their social lives and beliefs as pillars of life as outline below.

Humility (*Thiliakä/Thiak*)

Humility is the quality of being humble, a low self-regard and sense of unworthiness. In a religious context humility is define as being "unselved", a liberation from consciousness of self, a form of temperance that is neither having pride (or haughtiness nor indulging in self-criticism). Humility is the feeling or attitude that you have no special importance that makes you better than others. At glance, humility seems like a negative quality, almost like a sign of weakness rather than strength. In reality, humility is a type of modesty that will get someone very far in life as an individual person. Solomon (2004), describes ethics as quest for, and understanding of the good life, worth living putting every activity and goal in place, knowing what is worth doing and what is not in every decline (Solomon and Clancy, 2004). Nuer ethics lay much emphasis on the value of humility and individual persons expected humble to prosper in life as opposed to those who are proud. It's for this reason that the Nuer children are admonished to be humble for so as to grow and prosper in life.

The care for children is a moral responsibility among the Nuer society, training a child is to give directions on how to be responsible for future generation when he is fully grown up. The Nuer say; "train the children how to learn their ancestors used to live with humility. A Nuer child is train to learn ancestral ways of life, humble and respect others and to take up responsibilities for the next generation. The Nuer say "the child is trained for tomorrow" (*gat ngickɛjɛ kɛ ruun*). That is why, when a Nuer young man wants to marry, the background of both parents is sought whether they are considered as humble individuals and families. These trends of character assessment, among others, are incumbent in Nuer social lives. This wonderful indigenous value is padding away in Nuer society these days, with exception of few families who still uphold and preserve these cultural values. This social change could be attributed to some factors: interacting with other communities having different traditions and

112

migration of youth to foreign countries adopting new social behaviours that do not conform with Nuer ways of lives where humility and honesty are observed.

Honesty (*Thuok*)

Honesty is a facet of moral character that brings positive and virtuous attributes such as integrity truthfulness, straightforwardness, including good conduct along with the absence of lying, cheating, and theft. In some societies, honesty also involves being trustworthy and sincere. Honesty guides good people while dishonesty destroys treacherous ones.

The Nuer society considers honesty as one of highly cherished moral value, in which individual person is expected to be truthful and honest at all times. Those individuals who do not comply with the society rules of truth and became dishonest end up hurting someone else and themselves too. Honesty acts as the basis of trust and good relationships between humans and the *kuoth nhial* (God in the sky), who rewards those who maintain such values with prolong lives while those who bear false witness are regarded as sinful as the victims themselves. According to the Nuer traditional norms, honesty promotes a person to higher level of authority. It is also a basis of building trust, respect and relationship among and between members of the society. Reflecting to the past experiences on how a Nuer witness gives testimony in a court of law or before a competent body such as chiefs or traditional authority, the measure of such person is refers to personal honesty and truth worthy in the community.

Generosity and Hospitality

Generally, kindness is understood as the quality of being friendly, generous, and considerate, helpful and caring about other people or an act that shows this quality. Kindness is sincere and voluntary use of one's time, talent, and resources to better the lives of others, one's own life and the world through genuine acts of love, compassion and generosity. Hospitality is further explains as a friendly welcome behavior towards guest or people you have just met. It is a treatment of strangers and friends alike and welcoming one another into their homes.

The virtues, kindness and hospitality are highly esteemed in Nuer society. The Nuer people are known for their kindness and hospitality and more so to the strangers. These values are extended not only to human beings but also to other creatures such as snakes, birds, dogs and wild animals. The basis of this understanding is that *kuoth* (God) created all creatures and it is by his kindness that maintains and keeps everything alive. Nuer people believe that when someone has more children and cattle, it is being considered as blessing from God because of his good deeds towards others and relationship with God. The basis of this understanding is what we have already noted that kuoth (God) created all people equal and should have equal treatment for all. For this reason, the Nuer believe that those who abide by this virtue receive both spiritual and materials blessings.

Chastity (*lät cungni*)

Chastity is the state of abstaining from sexual intercourse before or outside of marriage; avoidance of sexual sins; the quality of being chaste; moral purity. Chastity is also known as purity, is a virtue related to temperance and commonly refers to the quality or virtue of refrain from sexual activity that's considered immoral, especially according to the teachings of certain religions. It sometimes means about the same thing as celibacy- refraining from all sexual activity, when members of certain religion such like monks, take a vow of chastity- the quality of being chaste also used in a more general way to mean morally pure.

The past theories that described Africans as immoral or even unethical have greatly contributed to the negative attitude toward the perception of chastity in Africa. The real situation however is that Africans command both men and women to live a chaste life. Faithfulness is highly respected in the Nuer cultural norms and the individuals and families who uphold it are honored. The Nuer observed chaste on how a person lives in the community by performing good deeds and acquired wealth through hard work in transparent manner without hurting someone or society as whole. For example, among the Nuer, a person who lives longer than anyone else is being perceived pure and chaste in the sight of God and the society. This explains the great emphasis that was placed on virginity among the Nuer community in the past, remains significance for ensuring loyalty and respect even today.

Loyalty, Respect and Protection
Loyalty is uncountable support that one always gives to someone because of his feelings of duty and love towards others; it is also a quality of being firm in friendship or support for someone. Respect is a positive feeling or action shown towards someone or something considered important or held in high esteem, it also means that you accept somebody for who they are, even when they are different from you or you do not agree with them. Protection is any measure taken to guard a thing against damage caused by outside forces, it is also activities aimed at ensuring full respect for the rights of individual in accordance with human rights law and culture of the people. Aware also, protection can be used negatively. For example, people may protect a person who has done wrong things to face justice before the law.

Loyalty is a national satisfaction of being real human being (*Nei ti Naath*), who believe that what they have as a people is enough to share it with the other nationalities. Loyalty to Nuer is an acceptance of dignity which makes it real nationalism, loyalty and patriotism, proud of their national identity. The concept of loyalty among the Nuer existed long before the coming of Turkish-Egyptian and Angola-Egyptian invaders to Nuer land (*Rol Naath*) in the 18th century. The Nuer were egalitarian - a way of living which constitutes culture, customs, norms and traditions of their ethnic identity which implies that Nuer, is a Nation with its nationalism and loyalty to itself. The Nuer have their own language (*Thok Nath*), customs, norms, traditions and mythical narratives which describe who they were as a nation. For example, one of the Nuer mythical tales is that all Nuer people were created in Bentiu in a place called Koat Liech currently Koch County in western Upper Nile State. This is an ancestral myth which is rooted into Nuer thoughts even today although earlier migration narrative gives *"kuer kuoŋ"* as the birth place of Nuer as a distinct nation.

Loyalty, respect and protection among Nuer people, all deal with issues of interpersonal relation, where one is expected to demonstrate such virtues to elders, parents, age mates, relatives, children and member of the whole community according to traditions and customs of the state. We have noticed above that Nuer Nation was homogenous state which they viewed as stable, peaceful and understand themselves and their laws and easily respect their rules, which are their own making and practice as part of their traditions and customs, exemplified by the Leopard Skin Chief. The Nuer requires individual to show these qualities as an obligation by tradition when interacting with other members of community. In the final analysis, loyalty, respect and protection are at large expected to guarantee the well-being and safety of all its members who upheld these traditional norms and values. If these moral values fall apart, the whole society is in crisis and this may lead to negative practices such as stealing and killing of innocent people as it happens nowadays in the Nuer Nation.

Theft (*Wän/kueel*)
Stealing is the act of taking something from someone unlawfully or without right or permission. It also presents use someone else's words or ideas as one's own, abduction of children, raiding of cattle such as what is happening in Jonglei State - South Sudan. Most Nilotic communities in South Sudan consider stealing as one of the sacrilegious offenses against God and humanity. Stealing is generally forbidden and those who are found to have committed such acts are severely punished. In the past, severe penalties were meted to a person who committed theft. Some communities declared death sentence to the thieves while other criminals were warned and ridiculed publicly (Getui, 2008). For example in Kenya, when a thief is caught stealing red handed in a mob, is beaten and burned to death.

There are certain specific situations which fall within the definitions of theft among the Nuer. When cattle are taken without any real reason other than that the thief (*wään*) wants to own them, the word *kual* applies to such situation. Cases where a person steals cattle from his neighbours merely because he covets them, the word *pec* is used to describe situations where superior force is used for example, when two communities are engaged in cattle raids the more powerful group raids the weaker or when the government seize cattle from the community by force, pec is used. Also the word mac, which means theft or misappropriation, implies deprivation by fraud or cunning or robbery, i.e. cheating. When cattle, sheep and goats are stolen, killed and secretly eaten by the thief (*kuel/wään*) this type of theft is known as (*luc yaŋ/cow or luy dɛl/goat*), the principle of compensation applied in such cases. Thefts that are related to material possessions such like, fishing -spears, hoes, and axes-all articles made of iron (*cut*) their scales of compensation differed considerably from community to the other. For example, the Gaawäär would demand six head of cattle for the theft of a fishing-spear. Lak Nuer would demand one cow only. The probable reason for this disparity was that compensation was conditioned locally by the relative difficulty of obtaining those articles, and also by the number of cattle paid for them in the first instance, the Gaawäär, remotely situated from the trade channels through which iron goods which were only obtained from the Anyuak to the east or through the Atuot Dinka to the west. According to Howell (2018), in lak country a cow would purchase a bundle of these goods but in Gaawäär the cost was much higher (Howell, 2018).

In the Nuer customs, stealing is considered as the worst offense that has severe consequences and penalties. Stealing is generally forbidden and those who are found to have committed this offense are severely punished according to Nuer customary laws and they are looked at as evil and worthless. In the past, the act of stealing brings shame to individuals and families. It affects social relations such as marriage even climbing to the leadership in the community. Whenever a known thief passed by one's home, it was acceptable to inform other neighbors to be careful about that thief and if anything got lost, he or she would be blamed for. Stealing is condemned because it deprives those who have worked hard and are entrusted by God with the property they possess.

In the contemporary Nuer society though, the situation has gone from bad to worse as the young people have lost humility their grandfathers used to enjoy. The youth at this modern age, have taken the laws into their own hands, theft has become common and daily practice as every young person has a gun, a challenge which in my opinion, will take some times for the government to put rule of law in place, to disarm the population. This situation has led to state of lawlessness in all the areas of South Sudan including the Nuer land. It is therefore, imperative for one to argue that communal fighting, murdering and killing of innocent people will remain uncontrollable by the law enforcement agencies in the whole country due to weak government's institutions.

Witchcraft (*tiët*)
Among the Nuer, the witch is the perpetrator which could be both men and women and are the people who bewitch people to bad luck, disability, and even death witchcraft is the action. Generally, evil eye is a look or stare that is believed to bring bad luck for the person at whom it is directed for reason of envy or dislike. If someone gives you the evil eye, they look at you with anti-social "evil eye" (*pɛth*), so that such person constantly kill people and cattle by looking at them, in an unpleasant way, usually because they dislike you or are jealous of you. Wizard is defined as a person who performs magic or witchcraft or someone who is particularly skillful at a certain activity. On the other hand, witchcraft is the use of supernatural powers, usually to do harm. Witchcraft is a mystical power by which some people are thought to be able to harm or kill others when they do not like them. Its related evil act is sorcery, the use of some material object for the same purpose (Ojijo, 2012). Witches and sorcerers among the Nuer have their roots in spiritism. It means "associated to the spirits." Witchcraft power is perceived as misused power and abuse of it. Usually, a person accused of witchcraft feels offended and denies it. In the common action of the community against witchcraft we find perhaps the only conception among the Nuer which even approaches the notion of criminal or public law. Nuer say that in the past witches of these kinds were often killed with at least the tacit consent of the whole community to which they belonged. Persons with evil eyes are also grouped with witches and sorcerers. Both of them are given inverted attributes which have some mythological figures in them. Someone who practices witchcraft or accused of doing so is called a witch. Traditionally, witchcraft is the exercise or invocation of alleged supernatural power to control people or events practices typically involving sorcery or magic.

The evil eye person sometimes known as wizard ''pëth'' is one of unwanted shunned act considered as harmful and most fearful among the Nuer society. The Nuer perception of a particular person possessing power of evil eye is derived out of jealousy of someone's wealth, health, success, beauty, appearance and includes fatness, despise and of being in disputes or different opinion with the evil eye person. The Nuer believe that coming into conflict with such a person makes them use such power to inflict harm to an individual or property. Such person is described as having red eyes that identify them from others. It is assumed that their powers are inherited from their ancestors although no definite known clan or Nuer section according to some Nuer elders, an evil eye person, carries out evil acts against humans and domestic animals which make people scared for their lives. For example, when an evil eye person passes by, and there is a healthy baby or anything of value around, people try to hide such object from the sight of the evil eye because they fear that if they see the child or valuable property, may lead to the child sickness or destruction of the valuable item. If anything happens later on, people will claim that the misfortune is being brought about or caused by that evil eye person who passed by earlier on. The evil eye person is being assumed that seeing such attraction will make them jealous and cause harm especially to fat calf or affect the quantity and quality of milk production. The peth might be killed without grave danger of retaliation and, if compensation was demanded, only six heads of cattle need be paid to the kinsmen. Although this is doubtful as there is no any record or traditional sources referring to such circumstances. Accusations of the evil eye are fairly common today, but I have no details of the possessors being killed in the past.

However, it is difficult to finger-point to that person as an evil eye only when someone has been tired of keeping this as secret for some time, then will now decide to name the person publicly which may anger the evil eye and call for a court case claiming being falsely accused. Because, sometime there is no factual evidence on this, the accuser will be fined with a cow unless otherwise, proving such claims with evidence from the community elders who know the background of the ancestors of the evil eye person or their admission will put the verdict on him or her. During my interaction with some elders from western Nuer, it was revealed that some evil eyes person or wizards may accept of being in possession of evil power and can inform the people to hide away anything of value or cover their children when they are advancing to your home. They can also choose to inform the people that never hide or cover anything of value as they do not intend to inflict any harm at that particular period, sometimes as a joke. Whatever the evil eye does, it has to be cured by witch craft doctor, who Nuer people refer to as (*tiët*).

The function of the witch-craft doctor (*tiët*) is to identify who has caused a problem to another person and provide the remedy to the omen by making procedural that involves invocations. If a child is sick and taken to him/her, may identify the person who has attacked or beaten by evil eye and will perform her/his magical powers to remove whatever has been inflicted on a person as a cure; sometimes, the witch-craft may name the evil eye or keep it anonymous. When such misfortunes occur, the head of the family visits a *tiët*, a person who sees past and future happenings. The *tiët* will relate the cause of the misfortune, the kind of sacrifice that should be offered and give instructions on how the rituals should be performed. The Nuer believe that their ancestors will also send messages through dreams and visions on how misfortunes would be overcomed and managed. *Tiët* is also concerned with warfare and cattle raids they work magic against other communities; to make the infliction of wounds upon them easy; to destroy or weaken their defence. An expert who performs ritual to bring about the downfall of enemies in another ethnic community acting in the interests of his own people. His action is beneficial magic to his own people, black magic to those of the opposing segment, and there is no formalized community to which both belong and which would consciously react against his performance.

Emergence of incest (*Ruaal*)

For several years researchers have been recording similar versions of two distinct origin stories maintained among communities that speak "Nuer", one for the Eastern and Western Jikäny confederations and another for everyone else. The Jikäny tale hinges on a famous ancestor named *Kiir,* known as *kiir kaker* (gotten from "gourd"), while the main *tuk nath* tradition centers on a famous tamarind tree. These legends seem incompatible because they raise different metaphors and name different ancestors. But according Nuer (*Naath*) customs about exogamy and incest, both fables carry the same meaning about making kinship through exogamous marriages. In the most rudimentary forms of the tale, two "brothers" named Ɣääk and *Gëë* came together under a particular tamarind tree called *Koat-Liech* on the west bank of Bahr el Jebel and at this sacred tree, Ɣääk and *Gëë* cut a steer in half (from head to tail) to prohibit "incest" (ruaal) between their offspring's. *Koat-Liech* is a sacred site where Ɣääk and Gëë memorialized their common bond by vivisecting a steer in this manner and declaring that their descendants could not marry one another anymore. They also agreed that this tree had mounted as a boundary between the "descendants" of Ɣääk to the south and those of Gëë to the north. Stringham (2016), opines that this tree was eventually burned down at an event that British authorities observed firsthand in 1918 (Stringham, 2016). Given that Nuer use the same rite to address incest that they also say marked the "beginning of people", (*tuk Naath*) as a story about redefining bonds of kinship and transforming ordinary "humans" (ran) into beings morally valid as "people" (naath) whose exogamous relationships made them Nuer. Nuer traditions indicate that Gëë and Ɣääk, were the first "people" (*naath*), descendants of "*Ran,* (human) whose father is said to be kwoth (God). They argue that human beings pre-dated *Koat-Liech*. Taken as a whole, these traditions actually declare that divinity created Homo sapiens (the species to which all modern human beings belong) sometime before Gëë and Ɣääk but that it was these particular ancestors who created meaningful history (*tuk naath*) by inventing a kind of exogamous kinship. We have noticed similar myth about Nuer elders inventing incest at "*kuer kuong*" at the time they started migrated south from Kordofan around 1700, but there was no mentioned of any specific place or sign such like "shrine" where stopping incest was performed, that people could easily refer to. But *Kuer kuong* myths felt short of indicating Nuer (*Naath*) were first created, which gives possibility for further research. In Nuer culture, sexual activity between persons of closer blood relationship such as marriage between cousins or between uncles and nieces, aunts and nephews is prohibited. Incest frequently gives rise to emotional disturbance, particularly when it occurs between the closest relatives who respect themselves. Some people develop severe conflicts as a result of fantasies centering on incestuous wishes. The experience is often so traumatic that it leads to intense guilt feelings and a lasting revulsion toward perpetrators. Such victims develop feelings of degrading and sin which sometimes create bad lasting relationships between and among the families involved incestuous acts and those who have had incestuous experiences adopt a permanent pattern of promiscuous behaviors.

In the Nuer traditions, children were oriented and advised during early childhood with whom to talk to, in matters related to sex when they become adult. Generally speaking, it's strictly forbidden to have sexual relations with a close relative among the Nuer. Incest is considered as a taboo, unwanted sin that brings shame to the whole family in Nuer culture. If this happens, by mistake or unknowingly, those persons who have committed this act of incest (*ruaal*) have to be purified through special ritual performs by Leopard Skin Chief who kills an animal either a goat or a cow, cut into two equal halves and pull apart by the culprits without seeing each other meaning they will not do this again. But this can also be performed using cutting of symbolic herbs known as kuol in absence of the animals, and more recently the breaking and drinking of an egg has been added mostly in eastern Nuer.

Murder (*Luy*)
In African communities in general, murder is totally condemned. The idea behind the prohibition of killing is that life comes from God and God alone can take it. There is no time therefore, when killing is justified. Those who fail to comply with the recommended rites are punished through strange death or other occurrences to the members of their family members. Death by suicide is general frowned at and considered a bad death. Individuals who kill themselves are usually denied the full rites to burial in some societies. However, when suicide is committed due to terminal illness, protecting the family, it is tolerated and even praised as an act of courage.

It is fair to argue that Nuer traditional religion plays a very important role in shaping the character of Nuer society and their culture today and especially in conflict resolution. For example, the Jikäny and Lɔu Nuer communities in 1994 were engaged in persistent conflicts that erupted in early 1992 where many people were killed from both sides and had resulted to peace conference in Akobo town in Jonglei State. At a peace conference, elders observed that the religious leaders together with traditional leaders from both communities in conflict, understood the concepts and the importance of Nuer culture in resolving conflicts through traditional mechanisms leading to sealing of the covenant and oath taking between the two sections of the Nuer mentioned above. That peace agreement was considered as one of the most successful and sustainable in recent past, "if there were incidences thereafter, they were considered as isolated cases".

It is as a consequence of this Nuer reality of understanding relationship with God that make the Nuer believe in equality of all humans and insist that all human beings should respect each other. Each person is responsible and accountable to God, making it relevance for all community to live in harmony. Nuer believe God creates all in existence and man must refrain from harming these God's creatures. Killing animals or shedding blood is considered as trespasses to the supreme law of nature. This argument is enforced by fact that when Nuer go hunting, he does not slay the animal while sleeping assuming this may provoke God anger as a kind of murder. Nuer will stir up the animal and latter chase it for kill. The idea behind the prohibition of killing is that life comes from God and only God alone can take it. So, murdering in Nuer is considered as a sin in the eyes of God and they believe that only when killing your victim during the fight is justifying as self-defense against the offender.

According to Nuer elders, the main reason why the Nuer do not like murdering in cold blood, except in self-defense or fight, is that the spirit of the murdered victim may continue to haunt the killer dawn throughout his life time. This can also haunt his children and close relatives and might lead to pitiful to other misfortunates. Murder in all its kinds among the Nuer communities is totally unacceptable and condemned. As noted by Getui, this custom is also important in other cultures, stating that killing a person even in, self-defense, by accident or during war is unacceptable. For example, among the Kalenjin people in Kenya, killing is still perceived as wrong. If someone therefore kills someone by accident and even if it was the victim who was in the wrong or in war, the one who caused the death is still held responsible and is expected to perform a traditional ritual of reconciliation which will involve the entire clan to appease and compensate the offended clan to reach covenantal arrangements (Getui, 2008). Once a covenant is reached, it must be implemented and respected by all parties.

Challenges in observing moral values
The questions about moral values are increasingly becoming a serious and urgent concern in Africa. In African Traditional Religion, moral values have always been associated with Supreme Being which the Nuer called *kuoth* and argued that moral actions stem from religion that comes from above. Thus, morality in African religion embodies the will of the divine being. The Supreme Being/ *Kuoth Nhial* according to Nuer is holy and omniscience. Since God is holy, He is morally good and therefore expects human beings to live morally truthful. As noted by Getui, the purpose of living in a society is to enhance human wellbeing for all concerned. Anything that undermines this purpose is wrong while anything that enhances the purpose is right (Getui, 2008). Thus, the moral values were either positive, negative or indifferent with respect to mankind. As we have seen from the above description, specific moral values and norms determine to a very large degree, how we live and relate to each other for better or worse. One can further adds that humans are best satisfied when we live with and relate to one another harmoniously that is what moral values and norms are about. In this last section, I outline and describe; moral responsibility, the Nuer covenant and implications of sanctions on moral values below:

Moral responsibility
First, it is necessary to distinguish moral responsibility, which is responsibility of a very specific sort, from responsibility more generally, including most of responsibilities within business and society. Moral responsibilities are those duties and obligations that are based on the rules and expectations of morality. Keeping promises is often cited as an example of a moral responsibility, (though keeping contracts may be more of a border line case). Watching out for the well-being of children is clearly a moral responsibility. Many moral responsibilities consist of responsibilities not to commit inevitability actions- not to cheat, lie, or steal etc.

Moral responsibilities unlike the responsibilities that define a particular role or position, apply to everyone, in every role or position, in other words, they are not part of any particular practice or profession but shared by everyone in society (Solomon and Clancy, 2004).

The Nuer salvation lies in commitment and corporate responsibility among the social agents of the society, based on shared wisdoms and responsibilities. To elaborate on this, chiefs, opinion leaders, youth, women associations and religious leaders including the Presbyterian Church of South Sudan's Theologians, Pastors and the faithful in general must commit themselves to serious learning as a life-long commitment. The knowledge sought and experiences include the values imbedded in their Nuer traditions. For an ethically sensitive Nuer person need not retreat from life into indifference but instead look for the wisdom shared by Nuer people in the past and seek ways to incorporate the same to modern lifecycle. My personal understanding, is that the majority of Nuer who received western education, tend to perceive the Nuer past as one which has no values is incorrect. Indegenous knowledge is essential as a form of social control in Nuer society due to the existence of a uniform system of education. Traditional education stimulates sentimental beliefs which validate norms. Normative education was a means of social control by which individual members of the society induced to conform to the Nuer traditional conduct as represented by their traditional elders. The significance of traditional wisdoms and responsibility among the Nuer elders shape the behaviour of the members largely upon their cultural educational setting. Ethically, the Nuer have shared wisdoms liken with biblical concepts: those who seek wisdom are, peace-loving and the same still relevant in Nuer society today. The moral issues in Nuer traditions are the measures of rewards and sanction in case of positive and negative performance toward the society and still very relevant for building harmonious life even in this 21st century.

The Nuer covenant (*Ngut Nuärä*)
In Nuer religious beliefs oaths have connection with rules and procedures. They are usually performed by the Leopard Skin Chief in a ceremony called in for this purpose. The Nuer use two forms of oaths: first, is *kweng*, or *kap tang* (to hold the spear-shaft) used in a variety of circumstances and second, math (literally means to drink) often employed in cases of unconfessed homicide. The taking of an oath is not an individual process carried out by one person alone. In Nuer religious sense kweng's ceremony demand both accuser and accused to take part and it amounts to something of an ordeal between them. In the latter, kap tang, where there is no known accused persons, those suspected and all their kinsmen are expected to participate in taking oath. In this ritual, the name kap tang which means holding to the spear of the Leopard Skin Chief, mostly the ritual is associated with the earth, and the ceremony amounts to a symbolic and sympathetic enactment of the process of burying the dead. In this ritual, a small hole is dug in the ground by the Leopard Skin Chief which represents the grave; over it are placed branches of thorny trees for protection. The Nuer place these usually over the newly buried deceased as a protection against the diggings of hyenas and other wild animals. Over this hole the leopard-skin chief puts his spear, while the disputants' squat on either side and place their right hands on the spear-shaft and each swears his innocence witnessed by all those present. It is believed that whoever tells a lie will be attacked by sickness and may possibly die unless corrective is applied. If either person falls sick he will hurry to the Leopard

Skin Chief, who reverses the process and thereby removes the contamination. Whereas *mäth* usually refers to a situation of homicide cases, where the murderer has not confessed or the killer is unknown. The leopard-skin chief performs this ritual by filling a gourd with milk from one of the cows belonging to the deceased person. Those who dispute their innocence are likely to drink of the milk. This performance openly defies the taboo on drinking or eating which automatically comes into action between the hostile parties in a blood-feud. There is sometime hesitation on this partaking, since it involves the victim's blood haunting the culprit. Since contamination is extended to all kinsmen of the unknown killer, it is doubtful that anybody would agree to take the oath unless he was absolutely sure of the innocence of all his kin men. This tradition is regarded as an important element in Nuer conflict resolution.

Implications of sanctions on moral values
In some global perspectives, conflicts and wars result to the displacement of people from their ancestral land and cultural changes that demand social responsibilities consideration and recovery of traditional moral values. Since advance of modern Sudan, Nuer tradition and culture have undergone dramatic transitions. Getui in her text, ''Responsible Leadership in Marriage and Family'', expresses that demands of contemporary society continue changing and propose ethical strategy such as: (a) African salvation lies in commitment to responsibility, (b) Morality of the leaders shall determine the behaviour of the rest of society (c) Religious leaders and the faithful must be without prejudice (d) Considering our past experiences, customs, ethical values and the world view, and (e) examining the results of our past actions help us builds on experiences for future living (Getui, 2008). Thus, building trust and confidence to regain Nuer cultural attitudes of minds is not an easy task to achieve in these modern times. Surely, we must understand the causes that have made things fall apart looking at alien methods of doing things; would not undermine the dignity of the people is one of the fundamental pillars of inclusive new development. The knowledge embedded in Nuer communities, among other relevant thinkers would guide their thinking as they enter the future decade of reviving the traditions, customs and norms. The power of wisdom should highly be understood, by Nuer elders and youth and religious leaders during this 21st century where many things are going erroneous due to mistrust, created by wars, conflicts and other factors that have eroded away Nuer cultural values once they deviated from the prescribed norms of behaviour to a culture of violence instead of peace and harmony. A situation, which Deng describes as a culture of "I know it", even if I do not know! This new culture of "pretense" is a real challenge he added (Deng, 2020). This is a challenge in which every sensible Nuer has a role to play in order to re-educate themselves; regain former attitudes of mind which conform to Nuer traditional ways of life as individuals within a community and larger community that used to take care of them.

Each person within the Nuer community needs to understand and be conscious of how to relate with others as beings who are rational, social and with a sense of right and wrong and that individuals are part of the whole community to strive to live the way the Nuer used to live in the past, meanwhile incorporating positive elements from other cultural, moral valves to serve them within the new modern setting which regulates behaviour of the society, amid new ethical challenges facing them. Today, the Nuer are faced with new ethical challenges that more often than not give them no time to reflect and thus take appropriate action. In such moment's community are forced to follow their make-ups. In such a case, the characters shall most likely depend on the depth of their previous ethical reflections. How well and how consistently they are ethical in their day-to-day living will be beneficial in occasions requiring immediate action in other words, the moral standards of their leaders both political, community and religious shall determine the behaviour of the rest of the society, through their past traditions, customs and norms.

CHAPTER TEN:
MULTI-SOCIO-ECONOMIC AND CULTURAL NATION

New wine in old wineskins

In the preceding chapters, social, economic and cultural life of the Nuer has been discussed. It is becoming exceedingly clear that however much the juggernauts of Arabic and western systems allure have been pressed upon the community, the Nuer would appear to have been selective about what to adopt and what to keep at bay. Despite the emerging modernization, the society has somehow transformed, through a track of social order preceded by a growing political elite and an affluent civil service that seem to control both the power and resources to ensure peace and stability, but the Nuer egalitarian system that has existed for quite a long time has resisted any foreign interventions.

In this final chapter, attempt has been made to present duality of life among the Nuer in terms foreign interventions and structures of administration, religion, culture, marriage and economy. In a global perspective, there are many ways societies organize themselves to maintain social harmony and power structures which address their social needs since time immemorial. These trends are found in ancient time where kings, emperors, monarchies hold the keys for power and social order in the past centuries. The emergence of modernizations, the track of social order has transformed, proceeded by growing political elites and affluent societies which seem to control both power and resources to ensure peace and stability.

In any system of governance which is sometimes understood to mean the traditions and institutions by which authority in a country is exercised; this may include the process of electing the government representatives, monitoring, and replacement. Second, it involves the capacity of the government to effectively formulate and implement the policies; and third, guarantee respect for citizens and the state for the institutions that governed economic and social interactions among the citizenry. The Nuer egalitarian system had existed for quiet long and resisted any foreign intervention aiming to make change. The concern of British Government for transformation was necessary to be undertaken by their administration at the time.

Although many Nuer were embittered by the massive military campaigns that led to their definitive defeat, nonetheless, they could do nothing but simply to submit and recognize the military might of the British invaders and accommodate themselves to the new administrative policies imposed on them. It was then the interest of the British Government to find a model that would be suitable for administering the Nuer people throughout Nuer Nation from which the Nuer District Commissioners (NDCs) were tasked to develop an alternative model, suitable to that of the Nuer (egalitarian system), in what has become known as "Nuer District Commissioners Meeting (s)": February 1st -5th 1943. Present in the meetings were: C.G. Davies – Governor (Chairman). Maxwell, D.C. Western Nuer Captain Romilly, D.C. Eastern Nuer; Lewis B.A, D.C. Lou Nuer (Pibor District); J.H.T. Wilson, ADC Western Nuer; P.P. Howell, and ADC Zeraf District (Secretary). The views of these administrators were that: the Nuer were now at a stage where planning for Nuerland as a whole was required, to lay a foundation for political development. It was also intended to encourage inter-district visits which culminated into first all-Nuerland Chiefs meeting scheduled for June 1944.

The main issues raised and discussed at the meeting were: firstly, the means of realizing Nuer confederation that would bring about all Nuer four districts together aiming at the same goal and when uniformity of progress and method on this is achieved would be the time to link the Nuer people. Secondly, the Nuer courts warranty; the Nuer Courts were yet to be established and that the problem of punitive method, where capital punishments, imprisonments and fines were seen as alien to Nuer thoughts should be grafted into Nuer system slowly, C.G. Davies argued. In agreement, Howell commended that the first step to be taken was the introduction and building up a sense of duty and moral obligation to the community, considering to the Nuer a federation which should go side by side with confederation. Thirdly, was procedure of court systems particularly to deal with the problem of punitive method referred to earlier, as alien to Nuer thoughts and that such ideas should be grafted into Nuer system slowly. The first step to be taken was the introduction and building up a sense of duty and moral obligation to the community, considering to the Nuer a federation which should go side by side with confederation. The last issue, was the appeal system to be set up, where Gatwot the lowest Nuer government representative pays over tributes. The Chief: kwar metot (sub-chief) or group of Gaatutni fall under him and has community police (chiefs' police). In Western Nuer the sub-chief can form a court and try cases independently, similar to understand is the case in Dinka Bhar el Ghazal region. But this was in disparity with that of eastern Nuer where cases go from sub-chief (Gatwot) to Head Chief and finally to the main court- Chief (*Kuär Buok*) who has a court clerk to: keep texts & records of court, presides at court meetings, responsible direct to D.C. for general efficiency of court work, and public security. This disparity was a concern and needed to be harmonized. It was agreed that an alteration of terminology could be necessary in the future as Nuer Political Structure develops. It was also recommended that the D.C., in his territory should not hear all appeal cases, but that a panel of chiefs from neighboring communities should hear appeals with the D.C. recording judgments.

 In light of all these attempts, two key recommendations were made: One, many D.Cs believed that Nuer were at a stage where planning was now needed and it was possible to lay a foundation for political development. Second, there was recommendation intended to have a number of Nuer inter-district visits to change views, coordinate and share experiences on both social and legal matters, which latter culminated to first all-Nuer and Chief's meeting in June 1944, which further proposed to encourage further Nuer Chiefs inter-district visits to discuss and resolve major substantial issues related to their welfare as organize system was then in evolution.

Adoption of Nuer management system
The Nuer have institutions consisting of social agents that have rules and regulations to settle their own disputes and beyond according to culture and customs with traditional mechanisms in place, some of these are outlined below.

Nuer community has a well-defined model of authority for enhancing peaceful co-existence and dispute resolutions (Nuer indegeneous conflict resolution). In their traditional settings there are eruptions of conflicts among them which they avert using cultural models. Traditional spiritual leaders were and are key players who arbitrate in cases of conflict. These leaders played a principal task in promotion of peace and harmony in the community since they are considered as the ethical professionals in their context of communal social life. The society considers them to act on behalf of Supper Being (*kuoth nhial*), living dead and ancestors. The Nuer society trusted them with cases as they reasoned for facts. There are always great expectations from the community about truthful presentation from the parties involved in conflict. Religious leaders are respected, trusted and looked upon on all matters of the community including addressing conflicts between persons, clans or communities. The leaders work together with government appointed chiefs and opinion elders in the community, take part in creating awareness to the society on the necessity of addressing causes and effects of conflict for the purpose of reconciliation and peacebuilding.

Different conflicts require different models to conflict resolution because every conflict has its own causes and occurs in given contexts. Within the context of the cultural and traditional system of the Nuer /Naath people, there is the goal of establishing 'truth' behind the causes of conflict between two conflicting parties in a quest for restoring social harmony. The key areas of conflict resolution that are found among the Nuer include: first, to stop the fight. This is done in the past by respected elders in the community, the spiritual leaders and now together with the government and the traditional chiefs. Once this is done, then call for dialoque takes shape. Second, in the negotiation ground, each party to the conflict presents their side of the story whereas the other side listens carefully for response. Truth is what elders are looking for from the conflicted parties as they give evidences which could lead to final judgment. Truth finding was/is done through the traditional cultural justice system where there is no deceit, or denial. People in both sides of conflict must be open, honest, sincere and transparent in their presentations. The Nuer believe that in a case where truth is not told curse comes bye. God's reaction and the living dead would punish the culprit or immediate family members or clan. Curse consists of certain words spoken and acts affects persons and the course of events especially when spoken by elders. The Leopard Skin Chief sometimes performs the rituals. Curse was and still used as a tool of discipline to all those members of the community who are not obedient to prohibitions. Curse is associated with traditional spiritual powers and because of fear to be cursed a number of people resolve to confess whatever happened to avoid being cursed. Curse comes as a desperate move after all other avenues have failed. Curse in the context of the Nuer community was/is essential for conflict resolution. It was a way of humanizing morality of the community. Majority of Nilotic peoples in South Sudan fear the elders' curses because they believe that they are nearer to God (*kuoth*) and almost joining the living dead who are witnesses to all behaviours and may take the curse seriously to act upon. Third is payment of compensation. There are different penalties paid by the wrongdoer to the offended family, clan and community depending on the degree of the crime committed. For example, part of the body such like broken bone, loss of property or life. Rules of behavior towards Nuer kinmen and neighbours upheld sanctions for good relations to continue, certain breaches usually reqire payment of compensation. Adultery required six head of cattle, bodily injuries's compensation was in proportion to the seriousness of the injury and there were complicated laid dwon in the traditions (Howel, 2018). For homeside, requires transfernce of fifty cows from the family of the killer to the family of the deceased, as a way to institute guilt over the offense in order to restore the balance between two parties involved in conflict. This process is the most painful experience of the action in the past as well as the present in the Nuer Customary Courts. At times, would demand the offender to be protected by the rest of the family members so as creates room for soul-searching and reflection on the importance of the harmony in the community. Fourth, *däk këthä. Däk këthä* is a sacrifice of killing a Bull by the offended immediately after the compensation if the offend was loss of life. By performing this ritual the offender and offended the communities are expressing and showing sign of forgiveness and reconciliation through communion and fellowship with one another, and with the living including the ancestors. However, the offending group does not share in the eating of the meat of the slaughterered Bull. The apology for the victims and survivors where each community involved in conflict was enough for the sacrifice that leads to assurance of forgiveness between the two communities witnessed by all the community members and their ancestors. According to Nuer cultural belief, witnesses of the renewed relationship are the living dead and the ancestors of the covenant. During this exercise the Nuer believe that humanity, nature, and God (*kuoth*) come together in unity and love with one another through forgiveness and reconciliation offering of sacrifice play a major part in peacebuilding. The blood of slaughtered animal used in the ritual is meant for cleansing of the two families or communities who have been involved in conflict. The traditional religious justice and reconciliation of the Nuer acknowledge that '*kuoth*' (God) and ancestors guide their moral order. In a case where a person acts conflictingly against the community's set restrictions, God react by sending misfortune and illness to those who violated the taboos. This is until appropriate actions are taken by elders through the traditional spiritual leaders to the offender. Spiritual leaders among the Nuer use rituals and have powers to address conflict. They are in charge of the community's divine operation in matters of conflict. Sometimes they become part of community elders. Conflict resolution involves spiritual leaders especially on its management. The role of Leopard Skin Chief in performing the ritual is very important here. He represents the living, dead and ancestors whom the Nuer believed to be part of the community. Ancestors are perceived to be active in the present life .Therefore, the living dead or ancestors address problems of both physical and spiritual world which affects the Nuer society. This is relevant to the Nuer as it gives ways to the elders and spiritual leaders to implement the covenant (*Ngut/Nguot*) that would lead to transformation of behaviour, change of attitude and reconstruction of relationship within the two divided communities.

Nuer conflict resolution model is inclusive with communal avenues that are dedicated to settlement of disputes. They have individual rules, which protect personal rights, communal interests and public morality; and they established traditional institutions which have served and continue to serve the roles of mediating, arbitrating, and adjudicating for peaceful existence among the Nuer individual members and society at large. In all conflict resolution mechanisms the essential focus is reconstruction of the broken relationship with each other.

Nuer cultural practices prevail over Islamic and Christian ways of life
In conquest situations and given the resources at their disposal, it would have been expected that foreign cultures would overrun the African practices. From religion, burials, polygamy and lifestyle, the Arabic and western practices remain mere alternatives the traditional Nuer ways.

Orthodoxy in Western Europe, or for that matter in the Christian world as a whole, has been fiercely opposed to polygamy in any shape or form since at least A.D. 600 and has shown itself particularly ruthless in suppressing the hated monster whenever it raised its head in their own ranks. Characteristically, today, many Nuer Christians continue to marry as many wives as they like as long as they have enough cattle for paying dowry despite the many years of Christian presence in this African region. The approach of the Church towards this practice of polygamy makes some polygamists to remain in their traditional cocoons and reject Christianity as they feel rejected and uncared for by the church which, ironically, bases her existence on Christ's ethics of love.

This question of whether a polygamist can be a full member of the Christian Church has received much attention in the history of the church in South Sudan without gaining any ground to the advantage of the clergy. This means that any doctrines against African practices will not succeed. Similarly, spirited campaigns against African religions that have been painted with all manner of negativity have remained steady and thriving. Prior to the advent of Christianity in Africa, the religious systems developed by Africans formed the basis of their religious, social and cultural life. Although this has been to some extent modified by colonial and postcolonial experiences, these indigenous religions continue to exist alongside and sometimes within Christianity and Islam to play an important role in daily experience. As most converts to Christianity are from the Nuer indigenous religions background, it is not uncommon to find Bible believing Christians in South Sudan reverting to unchristian practices from time to time, and especially, in times of felt needs and crises. Because the gospel is always received from within one's own cultural identity, those who leave Nuer culture to join Christianity take with them, in large measure, their cultural worldview which is heavily influenced by traditional beliefs. A convert to Christianity from a traditional background does not become a Christian with the same experiences and challenges as someone from another part of the world. Just like converts worldwide, Nuer converts' new religious practices remain colored by the culture in which they grew up. This is so because when people come to Christ, they are likely to interpret the Scriptures through the filter of their own worldview, thus often tending to be syncretistic by weaving to non-biblical beliefs and practices from past religious systems into the beliefs and practices of Christianity.

The first Presbyterian Church of South Sudan Missionaries who came from North America to evangelize southern region in March 1902, came into contact with this phenomenon of plural marriage; and they spontaneously qualified it as immoral. In their teaching, the missionaries put it clearly that for one to become a Christian he had to have only one wife. But, in a culture where polygamy was well established, this teaching gave no allowance for polygamy in any case; it rather put many in a dilemma. Although many felt the need to be converted, be baptized and join the church, the demands of the church on those who were polygamous, were difficult to discern and this has been and remains really a pastoral problem that requires "Anthropological model".

Anticipatory inheritance

Noticeably, anticipatory inheritance is an obligation in the Nuer traditions. When a Nuer young man marries, he receives a portion of cattle from his father's herd. This is referred as partial inheritance or anticipatory inheritance. Alternatively, his father gives a few cattle ranging from 4-10 and is called "*Thiok*" in some parts of Nuer society. This wealth enables the groom to build his home and form a basis of starting his livestock husbandry obligation.

When a girl marries, the groom's family pays the bride wealth in form of cattle. The number of cattle is negotiated, *tuoc ɣok* in advance. It is to be noted that young women are productive and contribute to the family in many ways. Some of the said contributions include caring for children and helping their mothers-in-law in form of marriage, the burden of losing a pair of hands to marriage is great. The Nuer consider the bride price received as a temporary replacement of the bride's contributions to the communal labour. The wealth received can be traded or invested according to the directive issued by the elder in charge. This payment of cattle made not only to the father of a bride by the groom, but also for the entire family members. They have to share the cattle according to the customs based on parternal and maternal relationships. The process of dividing the bride wealth among the bride's family members is perceived as a means of compensating the father and the rest of family for the loss of their daughter's household contributions and also considered as pro-creation. The cattle fill the gaps and cement the two families' relationship, whether the marriage is between the Nuer themselves or with other ethnic communities. The Nuer expression; *thilε nyal wei/wech,* loosely translates to mean that a girl has no specific nationality and that she can be married anywhere as the culture allows intermarriages with other ethnic groups. Despites the changes in inheritance, the Nuer traditional marriage remain an important aspect in building other relationships in the society. Nuer inheritance was and is always in the male line and includes: sons, brothers, half-brothers and then uncles as noted earlier on.

Cattle: the base currency in marriage negotiations

The notion of bride wealth in the Nuer tradition is integral to the entire societal setup and involves other connections in the community on how wealth is treated. Its importance is observed in various Nuer traditional ways of life. Among others, cattle serve in many forms in social relationships. For instance, close kin often form cooperatives to care for their herds experiences show that when the groom pays bride wealth, he must know the colour of the cow or Bull given and to which relative. Cultural practices dictate that he develops a checklist or a tracking mechanism for his cattle to record deaths and births. Traditionally, this tracking goes on until the wife gets four children or more. By then, the family is convinced that chances of a divorce have significantly diminished. Besides, after four children, the groom has invested his cattle because children are a compensation for the loss of cattle. The tracking also enables the groom to account for all his cattle including those born at the extended families of his in-laws. It is worth mentioning that if any cow dies or is slaughtered by bride's family, the hide/skin is kept and the groom is informed; a certification that the cow will not be paid back in a divorce settlement. Nuer relationships with cattle extend beyond human relations. The Nuer religion, for example, is concerned with relationships with various kinds of spirits. Some of these can form special relationships with individuals and their lineages or clans. The Nuer people dedicated cattle to particular spirits, which can be exercised through rituals that involve livestock.

However, Nuer custom has changed over time due to modernization and movement of people from place to place. The community's interactions with other ethnicities and urbanization brought changing values on formal education and Nuer livestock might have attributed for the changes. The Nuer traditional practices have undergone drastic transformation nowadays. For instance, modernization and immigration to other countries have led to the evolution of the Nuer customary marriage. Through my observation and experiences, cattle are no longer necessarily present during current marriage processes. Instead, the value of the animal is determined in monetary terms. That now, cattle paid for marriage in form of money which is called duänyni (lame cattle). This change implies that even though the community still makes reference to cattle during marriage negotiations, the element of future investment has been eliminated. As such, the tracking component no longer conforms to the Nuer marriage customs. Accordingly, the money paid during marriage settlement would be the same amount to pay back to the groom in case of divorce. The transformation in marriage customs implies that the money does not increase. Such changes will likely have implications on the Nuer matrimonial processes, especially with the value of currency constantly fluctuating ups and downs. Settling divorces may get cumbersome in future.

Resilience of Nuer religion (*käp ngääthä kuoth kä naath*)
This section describes the resilience of Nuer religion in conjunction with other African traditional believers. It is noted that most of the time, Nilotic, particularly Nuer Christians, seek comfort in their own religious symbolic systems, even though these may not correspond exactly to those inculcated and expected by their Christian leaders. As Magesa also observed, indeed these are often symbols and rituals that church leaders have explicitly condemned (Magesa, 1974). This description shows that the African Christian rejects remarkably little of their former non-Christian outlook. In other words, they do not recant a religious philosophy they were raised in.

Consequently, the African Christian operates with two thought-systems (Shorter, 1975). Shorter, further pointed out that the relevance and influence of African Religion in Post-Apartheid South Africa and beyond at once, and both of them are close to each other. Each is only superficially modified by the other. Okwuosa has pointed out to the writing in 1960 by the Nigerian, Chief Obafemi Awolowo, who made substantially the same point with reference to his own country (Okwuosa, 1977). He asserts that Christian and Muslim beliefs and practices are, with many Nigerians, nothing but appearances and social cover-ups: at heart and in the privacy of their lives, most Nigerian Christians and Muslims are African religious traditionalists.

Actually, Nuer contextual theology embraces other religious faiths in some of their traditional practices. For example, the Nuer may perform traditional, Christian and even Islamic marriages according to their customs. Nuer contextual theology live side by side with their high levels of respect to Christianity and Islam and many still retain their beliefs and rituals that are characteristic of traditional religions. Meaning the Nuer are traditionalist, despite their religious affiliations. In similar manner, Nuer traditional religion has its most solid element in traditional context and exerts possibly the greatest influence upon thinking and living among the Nuer people. The importance of Nuer theology cannot be down played, for the Nuer who are converted to other faiths such as Christianity or Islam still retain their dominant motivation for their religious life in Nuer traditions. Of course Nuer religion has continuously undergone many changes due to influence of Christianity and Islam, the impact is, at best, peripheral. Such was the case in South Africa at the height of Apartheid. The relevance and influence of traditional religion in post-Apartheid remained firm with mental images, emotions, beliefs and response in situations of need.

For the Nuer of South Sudan, the influence of Christianity and Islam and their impacts and memories of agonies cannot easily go away in the minds of people. African traditional concepts still form the essential background of many African peoples. Their innermost religious determination remains overwhelmingly African. For example, in South Sudan, many converts publicly claim the new intended meaning while unconsciously ascribing to them in indigenous beliefs. They come as people whose world-view is shaped according to African contextual theologies from which the Nuer religion is build.

The Nuer religion is an agent of social reconstruction which provides people with a view of the world, and inspires new ideas. This social change of the society keeps renewing itself to deal with the changing traditional beliefs. Many Nuer people still express high levels of belief in the protective power of sacrificial offerings and sacred objects. The Nuer believe in the evil eye, or the ability of certain people to cast malevolent curses or spells in most countries in African continent. Mbiti gives examples from five countries: Tanzania, Cameroon, Democratic Republic of Congo, Senegal and Mali where majority of people express this belief (Mbiti, 1975). Comparatively, like Berger and Luckmann, Mugambi are convinced that African traditional religion has an important role in the social reconstruction of a society as that of the Nuer. As both object and agent of social reconstruction, Nuer religion provides the world view which synthesizes everything cherished by the individuals as corporate members of the community. It would appear that Nuer religion is the most vital project for the people who are undergoing a rapid change as in post-colonial Africa. In Jaspers (1972), Mugambi is greatly influenced by Karl Jaspers' positive appraisal of mythical thinking. According to him the myth tells a story and expresses intuitive insights, rather than universal concepts. This prompts him to argue that a society that is incapable of making its own myths or re-interpreting its old ones becomes extinct. A vision of theology of reconstruction in Nuer contextual theology is a vital project of re-mythologization in which the African theologians should be engaged so as to discern new symbols and new metaphors in which to recast the central message of the Gospel in line with Nuer culture.

Understanding and observations of the current changes

Nuer community, elders, chiefs, opinion leaders are the societal agents of morality who can ensure that social ethics, rules and regulations that preserve society are maintained and properly observed. It is their duty as it was in the past, to see that all the members of the Nuer community uphold high moral standards. The societal agents are custodians of morality and therefore, these social agents reprimand individuals and groups who go against the accepted moral code(s). Though the Nuer moral values are no longer respected due to the changes that have taken place in the whole Nuerland, the situation in the Nuer rural areas has gone from bad to worse in modern times. This is a true reflection of the present situation that has created state of lawlessness in the whole of South Sudan as well. In modern setting Nuer people are only afraid of the youth and the Army. Few are concerned about the reactions of the spiritual leaders (some societal agents) such as: *Dak Kueth* in Lou Nuer region and *Makuach Tut* in Gawäär County, who now command great influence in social and political life in Nuer territories.(as shown i appendix 3).

Transgenerational identity and emerging urbanite lifestyle

It is now abundantly clear that the conflicts and intermittent wars resulted in emigrations and family breakups throughout the Nuer society. Forced displacement and migration often resulted in transgenerational changes, both for migrants and those who stayed behind. First, there was the war gainst British colonialism which affected all communities of the Sudan territory. Second was the cessation war from the Arabs north that was very destructive as the north used areal attacks on communities. Several communities took refuge in neighbouring countries. The refugees acquired new lifetyles and adopted different cultures. The third is the most recent civil war among the southerners themselves in quest for political space.

In all these disruptions, all other communities in South Sudan were affected and refugee status was an amulgamation of different ethnicities. Foreign influence sneaks in and intermingle with indigenous ways of life. The text is cognizant of the resilience of the Nuer's way of life through religion, leadership and marriage. Marriages that occurred brought forth hybrid children that eventually joined returnees as South Sudan citizens. What now exists as Nuer population over generations has deoxyribonucleic acid (DNA), a genetic material that claims its identity mainly through language. Although there are remnants of diehard indigenous population of the Nuer, socio-economy life and dynamic cultural outlook has changed. Since the enactment of South Sudan's transitional Constitution, issues are managed within the ambit of the Constitution and the Government of the day. It is incumbent upon citizens to submit to new constitution.

Meanwhile, the text has shown a dire need for national archives and museums to ensure that the knowledge of all ethnic communities is preserved for posterity. As South Sudan joins community of nations served by rapid communication system based on World Wide Web, the speed with which changes occur will remain uncontrollable.

REFERENCES

Alier A., (2003): Southern Sudan Too Many Agreements Dishonored, Ithac Press, 8 Southern
Court reading RG 1 4QS, Granet Publishing Ltd, Oxford UK.

Audrey I. Richards, (1969): Bemba Marriage and Present Economic Conditions, *The Rhodes-
Livingstone Papers,* Manchester University Press, Manchester.

Awolalu J.O. (1976): Studies in Comparative Religion, Vol. 10, No. 2. World Wisdom,
Inc.www.studiesincomparativereligion.com

Biblical Quotations:

New International Version (NIV), published in 1978 by

Biblica United States, Palmer Lake, Colorado.

New Living Translation (NTL), published   in 1996 by Tyndale House Foundation
located in Carol Stream, Illinois.

King James Version (KJV), published in 1613 by Robert

Barker in London.

Byaruhuanga-Akiiki, A.B.T. (1989 Eds): African World Religion. Kampala: Makerere
University Printers, Kampala, Uganda.

Davies J. (1980): The finite element method: a first approach. ISBN 0 19 859630 8/31 6
(Oxford University Press) UK.

Deng A. L., (2020): The National Dialogue: A framework for Sustainable Peace,
Economic Growth and Poverty Eradication in South Sudan Africa, World Book.

Deng M. M. (2012): South Sudan: Toward a Biblical Understanding of Polygamy,
http://allafrica.com/stories/201209040038.html

Diop C. Anto (1978): Black Africa: the economic and cultural basis
for a federated state. Translation by Harold Salemson of Fondements économiques et
culturels d'un état fédéral   d'Afrique noire. Westport, Conn.: Lawrence Hill &
Co, ISBN 978-0-88208-096-3, ISBN 978-1-55652-061-7. (Africa World
Press), ISBN 978-0-88208-223-3.

Diop Anto Cheikh (1981): Civilization or Barbarism. An Authentic Anthropology. Published
by Lawrence Hill Books. New York.

Duany W. (1992): Neither Palaces nor Prisons: The Constitution of Order Among the Nuer,
Workshop in Political Theory and Policy Analysis, Indiana University PhD Thesis.

Fortes M., & Pritchard E. (1940 Eds): African Political Systems, Oxford University Press,
Ely House, London W1, UK.

Fukuyama Francis (1992): the end of History and the Last Man. The Free Press a division of
Macmillan, Inc. New York.

Fukuyama F. (2012): The Origins of Political Order from Prehuma Times to the French
Revolution   Profile Book Limited Croyodon, London, UK

Garvey L. T. (2015): Family Structure and Kinship,
https://nuerinfo.wikispaces.Com/Family+Structure+and+Kinship

Gatkuoth J.M. (2022): The Parameters of a Traditional Nuäär Marriage, Africa World Books
Pty Ltd; India.

Getui M. (2008): Responsible Leadership in Marriage and Family; Action Publishers Nairobi

Kenya.

Gehman, R.J. (1989): African Traditional Religion in Biblical Perspective. Kijabe East African Educational Publishers Limited, Nairobi, Kenya.

Holt P. & Daly W. (2000): A History of the Sudan: From the Coming of Islam to the present Day Pearson Education Limited, Marlow, Essex.

Howell P. (2018): A manual of Nuer Law; Being an Account of Customary Law, its and Development in the Courts Established by the Sudan Government, Routledge 2 Park Square   Milton Park, Abingdon, Oxon OX14 4RN, London, UK.

Hutchinson Sharon E. (1996): Nuer Dilemmas: Coping with Money, War, and the State Berkeley: University of California Press.

Jal G. (2013): History of South Sudan's Jikany Nuer Ethnic Group, 1500- 1920, Africawide Network, Nairobi, Kenya.

Johnson D. (1994): The Nuer Prophets; A History of prophecy from the Upper Nile in the Nineteenth and Twentieth Centuries, Clarendon Press, Oxford

Johnson D. (2016, Eds): Empere and the Nuer: Sources on the Pacification of Southern Sudan, 1898- 1930, Published for The British Academy by Oxford   University Press, UK.

Johnson D. (2015): South Sudanese Past Notes & Records: Africa World Books Pty Ltd P. O. Box 130 Wanneroo WA 6065130, Australia.

Johnson D. (2016): South Sudan: A new History for A new Nation, Ohio University Press, Athens, Ohio 45701 ohiowallow.com

Kelly Raymon C. (1985): The Nuer Conquest: The Structure and Development of an Expansionist System, the Univeristy of Michigan Press 1985, USA.

Kristensen Brede W. (1968). The Meaning of Religion. Martinus Nijhoff, the Haque, Netherland.

Kitchener L. (1990): in the Government of Sudan, The Sudan: A record of Progress 1898- 1947, published by Sudan Government 1947, Khartoum Sudan.

Paul F. Knitter. (2005): "Religion, Power, Dialogue," in Magnus Lundberg (ed.), Swedish Missiological Themes, SMT, Vol. 93, No. 1, 2005:30.

Lewis B.A. (1944): "The Political Problem": South Sudan Archive, UNP, 66. G. 3/3- Juba.

Lienhardt G., (1961): Divinity and Experience, The religion of the Dinka, Oxford University Press, Oxford, UK.

Lugira (1999): African Religion. New York: Facts on File. Major Religions of the World World: Retrieved on October, 22, 2008 from World Wide Web: http://www.adherents.com/ReligionsBy_Adherents.html

Madut K. (2020): The Luo People in South Sudan: Ethnological Heredities of East Africa, Cambridge Scholars Publishing Lady Stephenson Library, Newcastle upon Tyne, NE6 2PA, UK.

Magesa L. (1997): African Religion, the Moral Traditions of Abundant Life, Mary Knoll: Orbis.

Mbiti, S.J. (1969): *African Religions and philosophy*: East African Educational Publishers Ltd, Nairobi, Kenya.

Mbiti, S.J. (1975): *Introduction to African Religion.* (2nd eds.): East African Educational Publishers, Ltd. Nairobi, Kenya.

Mbiti S. J. (1975): *introduction to African religion, Praeger, New York*

Ayayo (1976): Traditional Ideology and Ethics among the Southern Luo: The Scandinavian Institute of African Studies Uppsalla Offet Centre, Sweden.

Ojijo (2012, Eds): Luo Nation: History & Culture of Joluo (the Luo People of Kenya) People of Kenya)

Okwuosa V. E. A. (1977): In the Name of Christianity: The Missionaries in Africa, Philadelphia and Ardmore Dorrance& Company.

Pritchard E. (1951): Kinship and Marriage among the Nuer; Oxford: Claredon Press, UK.

Pritchard E. (1954): The Meaning of Sacrifice among the Nuer: *The Journal of the Royal Anthropological Institute of Great Britain and Ireland,* Vol. 84, No. 1/2 (Jan. - Dec., 1954), pp. 21-33

Pritchard E. (1956): Nuer Religion, Oxford University Press, Oxford, UK.

Pritchard E. (1969): The Nuer: A Description of the Modes of Livelihood and Political Institutions of a Nilotic People; Oxford University Press

Prah K. (2000 Eds): Between Distinction & Extinction: The Harmonization & Standardization of African Languages, Centre of Advanced Studies of African Society (CASAS), Witwatersr and University Press: Cape Town South Africa

Riam G. (2022): Christian - Muslim Relations in Sudan: A study of the relationship between Church and State (1898 - 2005), West Bow Press, Adivision of Thomas Nelson & Zondervan 163 Liberty Drive Bloomington, IN 467403 USA.

Shorter A. (1975): Problems and Possibilities for the Church's Dialogue with African traditional religion, Published by: Kampala, Uganda, Gaba Publications, Pastoral Institute of Eastern Africa, Pastoral Papers.No. 37

Solomon R. & Clancy M. (2004, 3rd Eds): Above the Bottom Line: An Introduction to Business Ethics, Wadsworth/Thomson Learning, 10 Davis Drive, Belmont CA 94002 – 3098, USA.

Stringham N., (2016): Marking Nuer Histories: Gender, Gerontocracy, and the Politics of Inclusion in the Upper   Nile from 1400 – 1931, Department of History University of Virgnia, February 2016.

Transitional Constitution of the Republic of South Sudan (2011), Juba: Government of South Sudan.

Turaki Y. (2006): Foundations of African Traditional Religion and World View, WordAlive Publishers Limited, Nairobi, Kenya.

UNESCO (1978): African ethnonyms and toponyms: *The general history of Africa: studies and documents 6. Report and papers of the Meeting of experts organized by UNESCO in Paris, 3-7 July 1978.*

UNESCO'S (2003): *Convention for the Safeguarding of the Intangible Culture Heritage: Adopted by the UNESCO General Conference on October Enter into force in 2006.*

Weche M. (2009): Bantu and Nilotic Children's Singing Games: A Comparative study of their value communication, thesis presented for the degree of Doctor of Philosophy, in the School of Languages and Literatures, University of Cape Town South Africa.

APPENDIXES
Appendix 1: The Tower of Babel (*Däpäny*)

Source: Gen 11:4

Now the whole world had one language and a common speech. 2 As person moved eastward, they found a plain in Shinar and settled there.3 they said to each other "come let's make brick and bake them thoroughly" .They used brick instead of stone, and tar for mortar. 4 Then they said, "come, let us build ourselves a city with a tower that reaches to the heavens, so that we may make a name for ourselves; otherwise we will be scattered over the face of the whole earth".5,But the Lord came down to see the city and the tower the people were building. 6, The Lord said, "If as one person speaking the same language they have begun to do this, then nothing they plan to do will be impossible for them.7. Come, let us go down and confuse their language so they will not understand each other".8. So the Lord scattered them from there over all the earth, and they stopped building the city.9. That is why it was called Babel (Babylon, Babel that echoes like the Hebrew word for confused), because there the Lord confused the Language of the whole world. From there the Lord scattered them over the face of the whole earth (Genesis chapter 11:1-9 NIV).

Appendix 2: Nuer Calendar (*Ciööt päthni Nuärärä) equating* English calendar

S/N	Nuer	English
1	*Tiop in tot*	January
2	*pɛt*	February
3	*Guak*	March
4	*Duoŋ*	April
5	*Duät*	May
6	*Kuor-nyuot*	June
))7	*Pay-yeetni*	July
8	*Thoor*	August
9	*Tɛɛr*	September
10	*Lath*	October
11	*Kur*	November
12	*Tiop-thar pɛt*	December

The Nuer calendar is twelve months, which most adult state in order as shown in the list of months given above. The Nuer count the months base on the appearance of the Moon that equates with an English name. Although, Roman months have nothing to do with the moon. Nuer months are divided into four seasons shown in the diagram below.

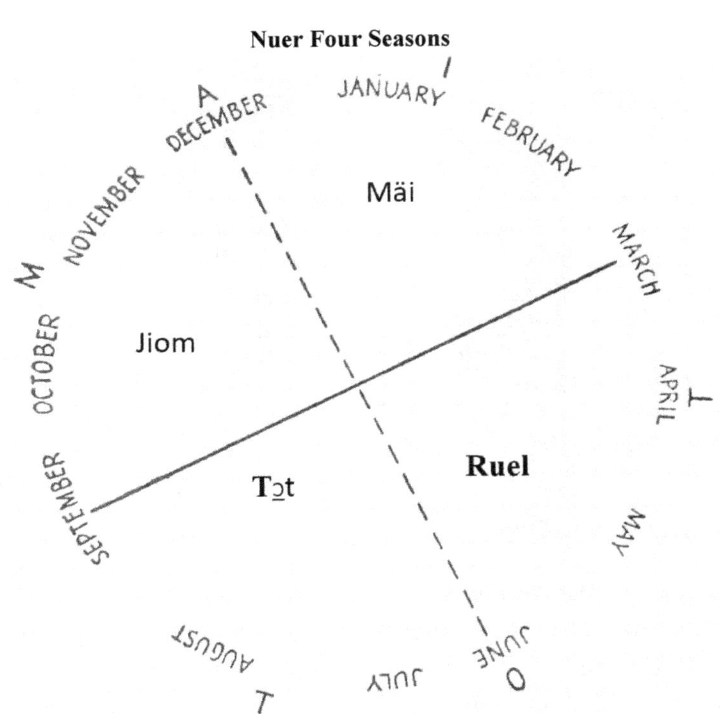

Nuer Four Seasons
JANUARY
FEBRUARY
DECEMBER
NOVEMBER
OCTOBER
SEPTEMBER
MARCH
APRIL
MAY
JUNE
JULY
AUGUST
A
M
T
O
T
Mäi
Jiom
Tɔt
Ruel

Appendix 3: Nuer Indigenous home grinding mills:

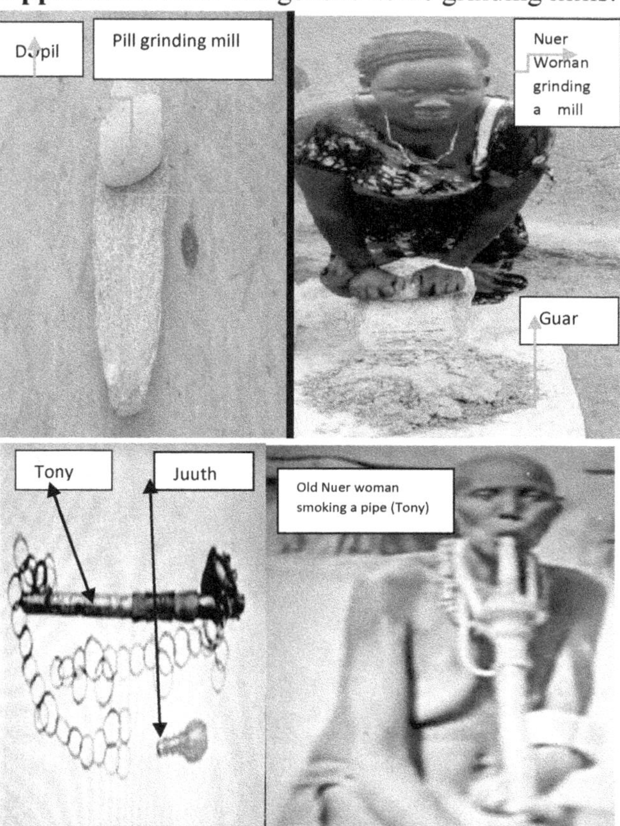

Pictures taken & organised by the Author

Contemporary Spiritual Leaders: Collected & organised by the Author

Appendix 5: A man with thick, matted hair with hidden axe (*jop), guor,* & *thiaw* discovered by Nyaguëc similar to what Latjɔɔr did in the past.

Collected & organised by the Author

THE END!

AUTHOR AND HIS MUM: CULTURAL CHANGE REALIZED

Photo by: Douglas H. Johnson, July 1975 –Waat.